South o' the Border

100% pure blue agave with just a touch of baby Mojave rattler!

By: Steven S. Long

South o' the Border

Written & Designed by: Steven S. Long

Editing & Layout: John Hopler
Cover Art: Paolo Parente
Interior Art: Paul Daly, Ashe Marler & Jim Callahan
Maps: Jeff Lahren
Cover Design: Hal Mangold
Logos: Zeke Sparkes, Charles Ryan & Ron Spencer
Steve Thanks: John & Joyce Goff, and the players in my *Deadlands* campaign—John "Dr. Marco Quadrelli" Grigni, Lisa "Faith Zion" Grigni, Jenna "C.C. Hope" McConnell, Harry "Charlie "Little Dog" Combs" Piper, Lisa "Vickie Lee Stoneman" Rich, and Todd "Standing Bear" Rich—for puttin' up with my somewhat erratic Marshallin' schedule.
Pinnacle Thanks: Shane, Michelle & Caden Hensley, Christy Hopler, Barry Doyle, John & Joyce Goff, the Listserv Rowdies, Jay Kyle, Jason Nichols, Dave Seay, Ray Lau, Dave Wilson, Maureen Yates, & John "Z" Zinser

Deadlands created by Shane Lacy Hensley.

Dedicated to all of the *Deadlands* players outside of the United States.

Pinnacle Entertainment Group, Inc.
P.O. Box 10908
Blacksburg, VA 24062-0908
www.peginc.com or deadlands@aol.com
(800) 214-5645 (orders only)

Visit our web site for free updates!

TABLE O' CONTENTS

HOLA, AMIGOS!

¿Como esta Ud.? Bueno.

Este libro es una guía a los eventos extraños y las personas interasantes de México. El heroe de Ud. puede viajar a un país con una cultura muy distinto de...

¿Qué?

¿No habla Ud. español? Lo siento.

I'll start again. This book is a guide to the strange events and interesting people of Mexico. Your hero can travel to a country with a culture very different from that which he is used to, meet interesting people, and get eaten by all sorts of strange new creatures.

Regardless of the language or culture, one thing remains the same wherever you hero may travel: raw, naked fear. The Reckoners have found some unique opportunities in Mexico's bloody history and they've made the most of them. The Reckoners have been busy south of the border; your hero needs to keep both eyes open if he wants to survive.

USING THIS BOOK

As usual, this book is broken up into three sections:

Posse Territory contains the *Tombstone Epitaph's Guide to Mexico*. This extensive guide, by the traveling huckster Charles Bascomb, explores the history of the Aztec Empire, the arrival of the Spanish and their conquest of Mexico, the land squabbles between Mexico and Texas and the US, and the current state of affairs along the border. Heroes can get the scoop on Emperor Maximillian, Marshal Bazain, and everybody's favorite one-legged general, Santa Anna.

Following the *Guide* is a chapter on making heroes from south of the border. There are some new Edges and Hindrances, a look at social class in Mexican society, a guide to naming your hombre something other than Juan, and two pre-made Mexican heroes..

No Man's Land contains a full chapter on making Aztec heroes. A shadowy underground of Aztec priests and warriors exist in Mexico, and your hero can be one of them—or one of their enemies. Learn how to make an Aztec warrior or a powerful Aztec priest. This chapter contains new Edges and Hindrances, new rituals and favors, some new uses for old Aptitudes, Edges, and Hindrances, and two Aztec archetypes. Either way your hero needs to keep a low profile—read the chapter and find out why!

Marshal's Territory has all the truth a gamemaster can stomach. Here you can find out what's going on behind the scenes down Mexico Way. What are Santa Anna, Xitlan, and *el Ejercíto de los Muertos* up to? You can find all that in Chapter Four, plus information on what those sneaky Aztecs are up to, the latest on politics in the court of Emperor Maximillian, and the truth behind all the strange happenings in the French Empire of Mexico.

A MEXICAN BIBLIOGRAPHY

Readers interested in learning more about some of the subjects discussed in this book can consult the following sources.

Bocca, Geoffrey. *La Legion!*

Brundage, Burr. *The Fifth Sun*

Caso, Alphonso. *The Aztecs: People of the Sun*

Coe, Michael. *The Maya*, 4th Ed. —*Mexico*, 3rd Ed.

Fodor's Mexico 1998

Geraghty, Tony. *March or Die: A New History of the French Foreign Legion*

Locsin, Aurelio. *GURPS Aztecs*

Markman, Roberta and Peter. *The Flayed God*

Mercer, Charles. *Legion of Strangers*

Miller, Mary Ellen. *The Art of Mesoamerica*

Miller, Robert. *Mexico: A History*

The New Bantam College Spanish & English Dictionary

Nicholson, Irene. *Mexican And Central American Mythology*

Vaillant, G. C. *Aztecs Of Mexico*

The Wordsworth Dictionary Of The American West

The Tombstone Epitaph's
Guide to Mexico

Sinster Secrets from South of the Border!

1877 Edition

A Word From the Author

Greetings to the readers of the *Tombstone Epitaph!*

My name is Charles Bascomb. I am a man of no real profession or qualification who, as my manservant Henson will no doubt tell you if you ask him, accomplishes very little with his time. My lack of obligations to tie me down, and the plenitude of resources at my command, have allowed me to indulge one of my few passions, travel. In my time I have traveled around the world, visiting places which are but distant fables to most men, and have seen sights ranging from the incredibly spectacular to the horrific.

Among the many places I have sojourned is the Empire of Mexico. For many years I have visited the land "south of the border," as we say in the Confederacy, to spend pleasant days with old friends and practice my all too rusty Spanish. The history, customs, and culture of Mexico hold an endless fascination for me which I cannot completely describe and have yet to completely satisfy.

The Esteemed Editor of this publication, Lacy O'Malley, is an old school chum of mine. Knowing of my interest in the region once called New Spain, and seeking someone to write about the area for his fine newspaper, he contacted me. While I am neither reporter nor writer, I could not deny the request of my old friend, and you now hold in your hands the exhaustively researched results.

As a longtime reader of the *Epitaph*, I must say that it is high time that it covered the lands of Mexico. The events and nature of what it calls the "Weird West" are not confined solely to the *American* West by any means. The whole of Mexico, which falls into the longitudes considered "western" by *Epitaph* readers, has been similarly affected by the changes which have swept our world these past fourteen years. Since *Epitaph* readers often travel as widely as I, a guide to the lands of, and goings-on in, Mexico will no doubt prove exceedingly useful to them. Even those who prefer not to travel in this often hot and dusty part of the world will find in these pages further verification of their, and the *Epitaph*'s, theories about the present state of our world.

In addition to such phenomena as the *Epitaph* often reports on, Mexico is the site of many mundane events of interest. The presence of three armies—the French, the Juaristas, and the Porfiriatistas—all vying for control of the country makes it a dangerous place to visit if you don't remember who's who and keep your wits about you.

During my time in Mexico I've run from bandits, drunk *cerveza* at tiny country *cantinas*, fought with one of the rebel armies for a few days, danced with the wives and daughters of the French nobility, and spent many nights watching and listening to people doing things they really didn't want anyone else to see or hear. I've talked to plenty of people, from disgruntled Mexicans, to Frenchmen who thought I was one of their own, to native Indians, to loyal Southerners down here for one reason or another. I am eminently suited to describing Mexico and her pleasures and perils to those of you who have yet to experience the country.

In addition to the more mundane dangers present here, I have sensed an unusual presence or threat which I cannot easily explain. I devote much of my report to an explanation of this threat, which takes some time to describe. It requires a delving into history and anthropology, subjects I am only partly qualified to explore to any serious degree. Fortunately I have had the help of a gentleman from the University of North Carolina, Professor Arthur Riley, who has lived in Mexico for years investigating its ancient history.

I realize that Mr. O'Malley did not expect a history report when he asked me to write about Mexico, but after you finish reading what I have to say, I have no doubt you will understand the necessity for the thoroughness of my explanation, and his reason for leaving it in this document instead of consigning it to editorial limbo.

Your obedient servant,

Charles Bascomb

Down Mexico Way

Desert and Jungle

Those of us who reside in the western parts of the Confederacy tend to think of Mexico as an extension of Texas or Arizona: a hot, dry country of red, rock desert and dirtscrabble living. That's not entirely correct.

The northern part of the country—including the states of Chihuahua, Sonora, Coahuila, and Nueva Leon, Tamaulipas, and Baja California Norte and Sur, which border the Confederacy; and Sinaloa, Durango, and Zacatecas, which do not—often fits that description pretty well. It's hotter and drier than Texas in places, and the linked series of canyons the Mexicans call Copper Canyon, which cuts across the country for almost 400 miles, is even deeper than the Grand Canyon over in Arizona.

Mexico has two things which regulate the temperature to make large parts of this region habitable: mountains and coastline. The altitude affects the climate more than anything; Mexicans usually refer to *tierra caliente* ("hot land"), *tierra templada* ("temperate land"), and *tierra fria* ("cold land"), depending upon how high up in the mountains you go. The northernmost desert regions aren't very heavily inhabited, but the closer you get to Mexico City, the more people you find. Many areas in the *tierra templada* seem pretty pleasant to me, but the regions along the coast have their attractions, too.

The Valley of Mexico

The heart of the Empire, and of the central region of the country, is the Valley of Mexico, a region about 7,000 feet above sea level right in the center of the country. It's about 75 miles long by 40 miles wide and surrounded by mountains. Five connected lakes, none more than 12 feet deep, provide water; sometimes underground earthquakes or volcanic activity makes them bubble and boil. Most of the cities in the Valley, including Mexico City, line the lake shores or are even built on land reclaimed from the lakes.

States in the central region of Mexico include Coahuila, Colima, Guanajuato, Hidalgo, Jalisco, Morelos, Nayarit, Puebla, Queretaro, San Luis Potosi, and Veracruz.

Southern Jungles

South of Mexico City the land gets lower and wetter; you find forests and better farmland. By the time you reach what they call the Yucatán Peninsula, you've got full-blown jungles, complete with parrots, monkeys, and jaguars. People accustomed to the dry heat of the northern deserts won't find the wet heat of the south much to their liking until they get up into the cooler highlands.

The southern Mexico includes the states of Campeche, Chiapas, Guerrero, Michoacan, Oaxaca, Quintana Roo, Tabasco, and Yucatan.

Mountains of Smoke and Fire

One thing Mexico's got which the Confederacy fortunately does not is volcanoes—*lots* of volcanoes. Two of the biggest, Popocatépetl ("Smoking Mountain") and Itzacíhuatl ("Sleeping Woman"), lie just outside Mexico City—and both remain active, though quiet. I've heard that superstitious locals believe the volcanoes will erupt soon, since they have seen the *hombres de azufre*—"brimstone men"—whose appearance traditionally foretells such catastrophes. However, Professor Riley assures me that the volcanoes show every sign of remaining dormant for the foreseeable future.

1877 Edition   "Believe it or Else!"   Only 10¢

Blood & Ash: A History Of Mexico

Here's that history lesson I warned you about. I'll keep it as short and sweet as possible, but you need to have some idea of how Mexico got where it is today to understand the threat it poses.

Mexico's history stretches back for over a thousand years before any white men came to American shores. The greatest Indian nations the Americas saw were established here.

The Olmecs

Our knowledge of the peoples who lived here before the Aztecs and Toltecs is scant, to say the least. However, Professor Riley has been kind enough to inform me about the most recent discoveries he and his colleagues have made down on the Gulf Coast in Veracruz and Tabasco. These discoveries concern a people the professors call "the Olmecs."

Not much is known about these mysterious people. At Professor Riley's best guess, they lived in the period 1500-900 B.C., and perhaps their culture influenced all those who came after them. What we know of them comes mainly from two types of unusual artifacts which Professor Riley and his comrades have found.

The first is a strange sort of amulet or figurine, made of jade, which the professor tells me is a stylized axe-head. These figurines have the shape of tiny men with large heads and babyish features. The mouths are deformed, with teeth which may be fangs.

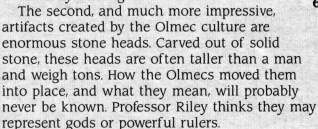

The second, and much more impressive, artifacts created by the Olmec culture are enormous stone heads. Carved out of solid stone, these heads are often taller than a man and weigh tons. How the Olmecs moved them into place, and what they mean, will probably never be known. Professor Riley thinks they may represent gods or powerful rulers.

The First Millennium

For the next two thousand years following the collapse of the Olmec civilization, until about 900 A.D., many different peoples flourished in central and northern Mexico, while the Maya (see below) established an empire to the south. In what's now the state of Oaxaca, in a place called Monte Albán, a tribe called the Zapotecs ruled. Their civilization lasted until about 700 A.D., according to the Professor's estimation; later, a tribe called the Mixtecs controlled this area. The Zapotecs are known for their underground tombs, only a few of which have been discovered, and their pottery urns depicting gods or spirits such as a Rain God, Maize (corn) God, Bat God, and many others.

Teotihuacán

However, the greatest civilization of this time was based in an enormous city in the Valley of Mexico called Teotihuacán. I've much to say about the place later on in this report, when I talk about Mexico City.

How did the Olmecs erect these massive monuments?

68

91

The Toltecs

The next great empire to rule central and northern Mexico was run by a people called the Toltecs, who lived from 900 A.D. until about the year 1150. The Toltecs were barbarians who came to central Mexico from the north or west. Their leader, Mixcoatl ("Cloud Serpent") settled them at Colhuacan. His son, Topiltzin Quetzalcoatl, moved the Toltec capital to a place called Tula, where he built a great city. According to legend, Topiltzin Quetzalcoatl had light-colored skin and a black beard, both unusual features among the early Mexicans.

As his name indicates, Topiltzin Quetzalcoatl was identified with the plumed serpent god, Quetzalcoatl, the most peaceful of the Mexican gods. His enemies followed Tezcatlipoca, Quetzalcoatl's ancient enemy, and a struggle for power ensued. Through divine trickery Tezcatlipoca brought about Topiltzin Quetzalcoatl's downfall. Topiltzin Quetzalcoatl fled the city, walking east until he reached the sea. There he set sail on a raft made of serpents, promising to return one day. The followers of Tezcatlipoca, unhindered by Topiltzin Quetzalcoatl's doctrine of peace, conquered most of central Mexico and engaged in much human sacrifice. They built many marvelous buildings and temples, and created artworks and craft items known all over Mexico for their quality.

The Aztecs

The eventual collapse of the Toltec civilization set the stage for the greatest of the Mexican civilizations, the Aztecs. Like the Toltecs, the Aztecs were barbarians who came to the Valley of Mexico from elsewhere. According to Aztec legends, their original homeland was a city called Aztlan.

Their chief god, Huitzilopochtli, told them to leave and found a new nation. They began to wander in the wilderness. Stopping by the mythical Seven Caves, they found a talking statue of Huitzilopochtli, which told them to go to the Valley of Mexico to an island in the middle of one of the lakes, where they would find an eagle perched on a cactus eating a snake. They followed his instructions, and everything was as he described.

Since the best parts of the Valley were already occupied, the Aztecs made do with what little food they could grow or catch. Their barbarous ways and savage religious customs offended most of their neighbors, but gradually they formed alliances through trade and marriage with the major powers in the Valley, such as the Tepanec Empire.

Eventually, with the help of allies in the nearby cities of Tlatelolco, Tlacopan, and Texcoco, they overthrew the tyrannical Tepanecs and established their own empire in 1428. Many of those who had been subjugated by the Tepanecs simply exchanged one tyrant for another.

For the next hundred years, until the time of the Conquest, the Aztec Empire gradually expanded in power and influence until it controlled, either directly or through the exaction of tribute, virtually all of what is now present-day Mexico. Tenochtitlan, which was larger than either Paris or London at the time of the Conquest, was so magnificent that the *conquistadors* who first saw it thought it a paradise out of some medieval romance. Mexico City now occupies that very site today.

Aztec Government and Society

The Aztec Empire was ruled, naturally enough, by an Emperor. The Emperor's responsibilities were to provide an example to the people with his austere and devout life-style, to control all governmental and military affairs as he saw fit, to assist the people in times of disaster, and to serve as *Huei Tlatoani,* or "Chief Speaker"—the chief priest of the Aztecs.

Assisting him was the *Ciuacoatl* ("Snake Woman"), or vice-emperor. Below the Emperor were two councils which advised him: the War Council (a group of generals who gave advice on military matters); and the Great Council (which included the most powerful merchants, judges, and officials, who advised the Emperor on matters of state).

A huge number of priests and other officials oversaw the day to day running of the vast Aztec Empire. They collected taxes, made sure that tribute shipments arrived on time, kept the roads in good repair, and enforced the Aztecs strict laws.

The Priesthood

Aztec priests played an important role in the government and possessed a great deal of influence and power. The priests were ruled jointly by the high priests of Huitzilopochtli and Tlaloc, though both men ultimately owed loyalty to the Emperor as *Huei Tlatoani*. In addition to their work in government they were, of course, responsible for maintaining religious rituals and traditions.

Clans

Most Aztecs never encountered their rulers or officials. Instead, they were governed by their *calpulli*, or "clan," with a common ancestor and profession. In Tenochtitlan, each *calpulli* had its own district or neighborhood. A *calpullec*, or clan chief, led each clan along with a council of elder men; a *teochcautin* served as chief law enforcer and head of the clan's forces in wartime. Each *calpulli* had its own deity which it venerated above all others.

An Aztec tzompantli.

Aztec Warfare

As a militaristic empire whose chief deity was a war god, you can imagine how often the Aztecs went to war. They fought to conquer lands and gain tribute, to destroy their enemies, and to capture sacrifices for their gods.

Stone Arms And Cotton Armor

Aztec fighters typically wore a type of armor called *ichcauipilli* which was made of quilted cotton about two fingers thick. It protected the torso and, according to the *conquistadors*, was both more comfortable and more effective than metal armor. They also carried circular shields.

Noble or special fighters wore *tlauiztli*, a "war suit" which covered the entire body. It was made out of animal skins or special feather-covered suits. A war suit was even more effective than *ichcauipilli*.

The primary Aztec weapon was the *macahuitl*, a narrow wooden club with razor-sharp obsidian blades set into the edges. These weapons were so powerful that they could decapitate a horse with a single blow! Obsidian-tipped spears and darts, often thrown with *atlatls* (a special stick used to throw a spear further and faster), were also used, as were slings and ordinary clubs.

Warrior Orders

The Aztecs had several warrior orders or brotherhoods which fighters could qualify for based on status, skill in battle, and similar achievements. Members of these orders received many privileges in society, and many were the only professional soldiers the Aztecs had.

The orders a warrior could belong to depended, first and foremost, on his societal position. Commoners could become members of the Jaguar Knights or Eagle Knights, two well-respected orders which provided a means for such men to work their way up in society. Nobles who captured at least five warriors could become *otontin*. If they captured many enemy warriors and performed enough brave deeds, they could join the highest order of all, the *quachic*. Most commanders belonged to one of the two noble orders.

Flowery War

When the Aztecs went to war, they didn't always intend to kill their enemies. The Aztec religion required many human sacrifices, so often the purpose of battle was to obtain sacrifices, not to destroy the enemy. Battles held primarily for the purpose of acquiring sacrifices were known as *xochiyaoyotl,* or "flowery war." To be slain in battle (or captured and sacrificed) was the highest honor an Aztec warrior could achieve, for it gained him automatic entrance into heaven.

Aztec Religion

Aztec religion is a vast and complex subject which not even scholars like Professor Riley completely comprehend. This report touches only on the relevant highlights of the subject, leaving the details for theologians and philosophers.

The Aztec World

According to the Aztec priests, the world, *Anahuac,* was wedged between 13 heavens and nine hells. The various heavens contained the all-important sun, the stars, the homes of the gods, and the paradises where the spirits of certain deceased Aztecs (primarily those who died in battle or were sacrificed to the gods) went. The nine hells contained various obstacles or challenges that the spirits of all other Aztecs had to overcome to gain entrance into *Mictlan,* the underworld.

The Aztecs divided the world into five "directions": the center and the four cardinal directions. Each was presided over by a god. Xiuhtecuhtli, god of fire, controlled the center; Tlaloc, the rain god, the fertile east (symbolized by the color red); Xipe Totec, god of spring, the dry south (symbolized by the color blue); Quetzalcoatl, god of knowledge and wind, the west (symbolized by the color white); and Mictlantecuhtli (god of the dead) or Tezcatlipoca (god of evil) the dark and terrifying north (symbolized by the color black).

The Aztecs also divided the history of the world into five "suns," or eras. The first, the Sun of the Jaguar, ended when jaguars devoured all the people. The second, the Sun of Wind, ended when fierce winds blew everything away and turned people into monkeys. The third, the Sun of Rain, ended when fire destroyed everything and turned people into turkeys. The fourth, the Sun of Water, ended when all the water in the sky fell, drowning everyone and turning people into fish. The world is now in the Fifth Sun, the Sun of Motion, which will end in a series of earthquakes, and *tzitzimime,* a sky demon, will descend and devour mankind.

Gods Of The Aztecs

The three chief gods of the Aztecs were Huitzilopochtli, Tezcatlipoca, and Quetzalcoatl. Which one was supreme depends on whom you ask and what sources you read.

Huitzilopochtli ("Blue Hummingbird of the South") was the Aztec god of war. He also represented the sun and the Aztec people in general. Hummingbirds and eagles were his animals. Most depictions of him show him in full war regalia, with the upper half of his face painted black. He carries the *xiuhcoatl* ("Fire Serpent"), a fearsome and irresistible weapon.

Tezcatlipoca ("Smoking Mirror") was the god of darkness, evil, sorcery, night, cold, sin, and the unknown, and the implacable enemy of Quetzalcoatl. Jaguars and turkeys are his representatives. His face is painted gold with three black stripes, he carries a shield and darts, and one of his feet has been severed and replaced with a sacred obsidian mirror. He wears another obsidian mirror at his temple. These mirrors are used for divination; in them Tezcatlipoca can see anything.

Quetzalcoatl ("Feathered Serpent") was the god of knowledge, wisdom, learning, culture, the Morning Star, and the wind. His animal is the quetzal bird. He typically appears wearing a red mask with a hooked nose (under which his face is white). He also has a black beard, and carries a star-studded scepter. Unlike most Aztec gods, he abhors human sacrifice; only rarely are they made to him.

Coatlicue ("Serpent Skirt") is one of many Aztec earth goddesses. She wears a skirt of serpents, a necklace of human hearts and hands with a skull pendant, and her feet and hands are clawed. Huitzilopochtli and many other gods are her children.

Mictlantecuhtli ("Lord of the Place of the Dead") is the god of death and ruler of the Aztec underworld. He wears a garment of human bones, and his mask is made from a human skull. The bat, spider, and owl, all of whom are animals of ill omen (especially the latter), are sacred to him.

Tlaloc was the god of rain and agriculture. Children were sacrificed to him by drowning; the more the children cried during the ceremony, the better the rains were likely to be. In appearance he is terrifying, with bulging eyes, fangs, and bluish or blackish skin. Despite this fearsome demeanor, he presides over Tlalocan, one of the Aztec heavens. His wife, *Chalchiutlicue* ("Lady of the Jade Skirts"), was also a deity of water and rain.

Tlazolteotl ("Lady of Filth"), another earth goddess, was portrayed as the goddess of sin. Although she often inspired sins, Aztecs confessed their sins to her and she "ate" them, making her important in many rites and rituals. She is often depicted as monstrous, or wearing a human skin, and she has a white cotton headdress on her head.

Xipe Totec ("Our Lord the Flayed One") was the god of springtime, and of jewelers. His sacred animal is the spoon bird. He resembles Tezcatlipoca, but his face is red and yellow instead of gold and black, and he lacks the obsidian mirror in place of a severed foot. Victims were sacrificed to him by being skinned alive; the priests would then wear the skin as a symbol of the rebirth of the earth in springtime. Sometimes the god himself is depicted as wearing a human skin.

Xiuhtecuhtli ("God of Fire") was the god of fire. Oldest of the gods, he appeared as a wrinkled, ancient man with a beard (denoting wisdom). He sometimes carried the *xiuhcoatl* as well.

Aztec Temples

Aztec temples are stepped pyramids of distinctive appearance. Few remain intact, for the Spanish destroyed most of them. A staircase went up one side of the pyramid. On the top of the pyramid was usually placed a small house-like structure. In front of this was an altar where sacrifices were performed.

Human Sacrifice

According to Aztec thought, the reason for man's existence was to provide the gods with the food they needed to survive—human hearts and human blood. Thus, human sacrifice was an important part of their savage religion.

Ordinary people often sacrificed drops of their own blood by drawing a cactus thorn or fish spine through their earlobes, fingers, or other parts of their body to request the aid of the gods. However, many sacrifices were more spectacular and bloody than that. Typically the victim, usually a captive or slave, would be walked up the stairs to the altar. There the priests would bend him over the altar and rip open his chest with a knife made of flint (*tecpatl*) or obsidian (*iztli*). Then the victim's living heart would be torn from his breast, placed in a carved stone bowl, and burned while the body was toppled down the stairs and to the ground. The family of the warrior who captured the victim would then take the body home, cook it, and eat it. The victim's skull would be added to a *tzompantli* ("skull rack") near the temple.

Many other methods of sacrifice were used. Sacrifices to Tlaloc, and sometimes to Quetzalcoatl, were drowned. Those to Xipe Totec were flayed, while Xiuhtecuhtli's were burned to death. Sometimes the sacrifices were slain in ritual combat where they had only false weapons to defend themselves.

Sacrifices were performed on various holidays and festivals, to commemorate special events, and to seek the favor of the gods. When the Great Temple which occupied the center of Tenochtitlan was dedicated in 1487, 20,000 victims were sacrificed in a four-day nonstop orgy of blood. When the Spaniards came to the city in 1519, the skull rack near the Great Temple held 136,000 skulls.

As I walk through Mexico City, I often feel a strange, disquieting sensation near where I believe the Great Temple once stood. While I am no believer in spiritualism or the stranger disciplines of the occult, I believe that the spirits of the victims of this horrible "religious" practice linger here still, bearing great malice for the living. Such would certainly be no stranger than many things that now exist in the world but once were thought myths.

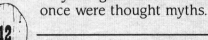

The Tombstone Epitaph's Guide to Mexico

Aztec Sorcery

According to the reports of the *conquistadores*, the Aztecs practiced some kind of sorcery. However, being devout Christians, they provide few details, and apparently destroyed all of the sorcerous paraphernalia and writings they discovered.

My own investigations have uncovered little; the Mexican people seem very reluctant to discuss this subject. As far as I can tell, Aztec sorcerers, who seem to have been devotees of Tezcatlipoca, possessed many different powers. These include the ability to change shape, cause or cure illness, cast curses, and foretell the future.

108

Aztec Calendars

Keeping track of time was of great importance to the Aztecs, and often held religious significance. Every hour of the day and night had its patron god.

The Aztecs actually kept two different calendars. The first, a secular calendar, had 18 months of 20 days each, plus five *nemontemi*, or "useless days" (unlucky days), at the end of the year, for a total of 365 days. The first day of the Aztec secular year was our February 2.

The Aztecs also kept a religious calendar, which marked days with 13 numbers and 20 day-signs such as Crocodile, Grass, Vulture, Motion, and Flint. Thus, a religious day might be 3 Rabbit, 12 Death, 8 Jaguar, or 1 Monkey. Each number-sign combination was associated with particular qualities and omens which governed persons born on that day. Being born on one of the *nemontemi* was considered an ill omen, and these people were considered cursed with bad luck.

The same religious day corresponded with the same secular day only once every 52 years, so that period of time held incredibly great significance for the Aztecs (much like the turn of a century would for us). A New Fire Ceremony was held wherein the old altar fires, which had burned continuously for the past 52 years, were extinguished and new fires lit. Furthermore, all other fires throughout the land would be extinguished and then relit from sparks carried from a sacred fire lit by the priests on the Hill of the Star near Tenochtitlan.

The Maya

The other great Indian civilization for which Mexico is known is the Maya, about whom we know much less. Professor Riley tells me that the Maya lived in the south, on the Yucatán Peninsula and nearby areas, but that their civilization had died out by about the year 1000 A.D. Many of their ruins are still covered by jungle, but Professor Riley assures me that archaeological investigations are underway.

The Conquest Of Mexico

Hernan Cortés arrived on the Gulf Coast of Mexico in 1519, where he founded the city of Veracruz. Unfortunately for the Aztecs, Cortés was a white man with a black beard who came from the eastern sea, so they believed he was Topiltzin-Quetzalcoatl, returned at long last. Montezuma II, Emperor of the Aztecs, sent many gifts, including ambassadors willing to offer their lives to the gods as sustenance, should it

Sneaking up on a bandito is seldom a good idea

be desired. The Spaniards terrified the Aztecs with their cannons and "two-headed monsters" (men on horseback).

Montezuma tried to keep the Spaniards away with sorcery and treachery, but all his efforts failed. Cortés and his 500 soldiers marched across Mexico, along the way acquiring as allies many tribes who were tired of being forced to pay tribute to the Aztecs. When they arrived at Tenochtitlan, they were formally welcomed and treated with courtesy. In return, the Spaniards stole gold from the Aztecs and held Montezuma hostage.

When Cortés left for the coast to battle some Spanish rivals, his second in command gave the Aztecs permission to celebrate the Feast of Huitzilopochtli. However, the assembled warriors frightened the Spaniards, who attacked. They killed dozens of nobles, and then barricaded themselves in Montezuma's palace.

When Cortés returned with 1,000 reinforcements, the Aztecs ambushed him. They fought for days. The Spaniards finally decided to escape down one of the causeways on a rainy night, carrying all the gold they could.

69

The Aztecs saw them and attacked. Nearly three out of four Spaniards died that night; many drowned when they fell in the lake and could not stand up again because of the weight of the gold they carried. The Spanish came to call this *La Noche Triste* ("the Sad Night").

The Spanish soon returned. They laid siege to Tenochtitlan. After 80 days the Aztecs surrendered and submitted to Mexican rule.

The Colonial Period

Cortés established a capital for his nation of New Spain on the site of what used to be Tenochtitlan. Today, we call it Mexico City. After filling in the lagoons, he knocked down the Aztec buildings and temples and built a few of his own—places like the National Palace, Cathedral of Mexico, and a convent for the Franciscan friars who arrived to convert the Aztecs to Catholicism. After learning Nahuatl, the Aztec language, the friars were able to convert many Aztecs, and at the same time to learn a lot about their culture.

In order to fully exploit the resources of New Spain—which included the Aztecs—the Spaniards established a system they called *encomienda*. Under the *encomienda* system, Spanish settlers received a grant of land which came with a group of Aztecs. The Aztecs were to work for their *encomiendero*, while he was supposed to look out for their interests and Christianize them. In truth, though, the Aztecs usually became nothing but slaves who labored to leech the wealth out of New Spain for their masters. Intermingling between Spaniard and native soon produced a class of mixed-bloods called *mestizos*.

During the colonial period, a viceroy appointed by the Spanish crown ruled New Spain. This soon led to discontent over taxes, the unequal treatment of native-born Spaniards versus those born in the mother country, and many other issues. Although it was a long time in coming—nearly 300 years—eventually the Mexicans decided they'd had enough. It was time for Mexican independence, and a new and bloody chapter in Mexican history.

Viva La Revolucion!...

When Napoleon conquered Spain in 1808, the Mexicans refused to obey a French ruler (little did they know what was to come fifty years later). In 1810, led at first by Father Miguel Hidalgo and later by Father Jose Morelos and Augustín Iturbide, the rebels fought an 11-year war of independence. In 1821 they won and established an independent monarchy. That didn't last long; Iturbide soon declared himself Emperor.

He didn't last long either. A young army officer by the name of Antonio López de Santa Anna Perez de Lebron led a revolt which overthrew him. He was expelled from Mexico; when he returned, Iturbide was shot by a firing squad.

70

Mexico's supposed "republic" period began in 1824 with a constitution and government modeled on those of the United States. Between then and 1855, it had over two dozen presidents. The one and only Santa Anna, who became a great hero to his people, served in that office not once, but 11 times. It may be that he has his sights set there again.

The Tombstone Epitaph's Guide to Mexico

1877 Edition   "Believe it or Else!"   Only 10¢

...But Not When It's The Texans

At that time, Mexico was much larger than it is today. It included not only what we think of as Mexico these days, but Texas, California, and what are now the states of New Mexico, Arizona, Colorado, Utah, and Nevada.

In 1829, President Guerrero abolished slavery in Mexico. That didn't sit well with the Texans. Then, in 1835, President Santa Anna decided to abolish the 1824 constitution and establish a new one which gave him more authority. The Texans liked that even less—in fact, they disliked it so much, they declared independence. They were determined not to let Mexicans tell them what they could and couldn't do. Mexican forces sent in to stop them met armed resistance (surely they expected no less from Texans?). The Texans captured Goliad and, after a siege, San Antonio. In a one on one fair fight, the Mexicans couldn't stand up to Texans.

Santa Anna was infuriated. He marched north with 6,000 men to crush the Texas rebellion. When he approached San Antonio in February, 1836 with half of his army, the Texans withdrew, leaving only 150 men (plus 32 American volunteers) commanded by William Travis in an old Franciscan mission—the Alamo. It took Santa Anna and his men ten days to defeat those 182 Texans. When he finally broke in, he killed every man in the Alamo, including Davy Crockett and Jim Bowie.

His good fortune was short-lived. Following a couple more victories, including one near Goliad where he had 365 Texan prisoners shot, he and his 1,400 men were attacked near the San Jacinto River by Gen. Sam Houston and defeated. The "Napoleon of Mexico" lost his left leg in the battle; after it was badly injured, it was amputated below the knee. He was captured and forced to sign peace treaties.

When returned to Mexico in disgrace, he retired to his *hacienda*—but not before having an elaborate state funeral for his amputated limb. Bishops, ambassadors, and other foreign dignitaries attended the ceremony at which his leg was laid to rest. Whenever his loyalty to the Mexican people was questioned, Santa Anna silenced his critics by reminding them of the limb he lost defending the republic.

I wonder if it would not have been better for him to have died in the fighting; it would certainly have spared the Confederacy much present trouble. Mexico refused to recognize Texas' independence.

Mexican troops assault the Alamo.

The Tombstone Epitaph's Guide to Mexico

Between The Wars

Santa Anna's retirement didn't last long. In 1838, the French, angered over Mexico's refusal to pay debts, bombarded and occupied Veracruz. Santa Anna was given command of the Mexican troops and forced the French back into their ships, giving Mexico the chance to renegotiate the debt. This victory returned him to grace. A military revolt in 1841 made him dictator, but he was ousted in turn in 1844 and fled to Cuba.

The Mexican-American War

Although it hadn't moved to retake Texas, Mexico objected when the United States offered Texas statehood in 1844. Tensions rose, and in 1846 the two countries went to war. A quick string of American victories followed. Hoping for a

114

quick end to the war, the Americans contacted Santa Anna and offered to sneak him back into Mexico if he'd help negotiate a peace on United States terms. He agreed, but after they got him back home, he forgot all about that little promise. Santa Anna soon recruited an army of 20,000 and was "elected" President of Mexico yet again. Needless to say, the US government wasn't too pleased with this turn of events.

Santa Anna fought Gen. Zachary Taylor to a standstill at the Battle of Buena Vista, but lost badly at Cerro Gordo. He retreated to Mexico City, but after the Americans attacked in force, he left it behind as well. His army disintegrated and he was captured and exiled to the lovely island of Jamaica. The 1848 Treaty of Guadalupe Hidalgo ended the war and gave most of Mexico's territory north of the present Mexican-Confederate border to the United States. This would have ended most general's careers, but not Santa Anna's.

Mexico, 1877

1. Mexico City
2. Matamoros
3. Querétaro
4. Guanajuato
5. San Luis Potosí
6. Guadalajara
7. Colima
8. Monterrey
9. Chihuahua
10. Veracruz
11. Tampico

Gulf of Mexico

Pacific Ocean

You Can't Keep A Good Man Down

Mexico hadn't seen the last of Santa Anna, not by a long shot. After the Mexican-American War, various revolts and uprisings continued to plague the country. In 1853, Santa Anna was invited back into Mexico to assume the presidency and bring peace. The men who brought him back figured they could keep him under control—but unfortunately, they died not long after that. Santa Anna took the title His Most Serene Highness and returned to his old despotic ways. To finance his army, he sold a little chunk of land that's now part of Arizona to the United States for ten million dollars.

Nobody in Mexico was pleased about that. They'd already lost about half their land to the Americans, and now Santa Anna was selling them more. In 1855, the Revolution of Ayutla deposed him, and he fled once again.

The Juarez Reforms

A full-blooded Zapotec Indian from Oaxaca, Benito Juárez, was one of the key figures in the Ayutla rebellion. He became Minister of Justice in the new government. The changes instituted by him and the other reformists, most of whom struck at the power of the upper classes and the Church, sparked further uprisings and revolts. Soon Mexico had two governments: one lead by Juárez and based in Veracruz; and a more "traditional" regime based in Mexico City.

The "War of the Reform" between the two sides ended in 1860 with a victory for Juárez's side. Unfortunately, it left the country desolate and poor—and that opened the door for the French.

The French Conquest

With so little money and so many debts to pay, Mexico decided to halt payments on foreign debts for a while. The British, French, and Spanish didn't care for that idea much. The three European powers agreed to get their money by force. They invaded Mexico in 1861, well aware that since the United States was busy fighting the Confederates, it couldn't enforce its "Monroe Doctrine" and help Mexico keep them out. The invaders occupied Veracruz, but the Spanish and British withdrew after a few months.

Not so the French. They liked it in Mexico and decided to stay. A French army of 6,500 marched on Mexico City, but were handed a humiliating defeat by General Ignacio Zaragoza and Brigadier General Porfirio Díaz at Puebla on May 5, 1862. But a year later, with 30,000 reinforcements, including members of the feared French Foreign Legion, the French occupied Mexico City, effectively taking control of the country from Juárez, who fled to the west and north. General Díaz and his men, knowing they couldn't hope to defeat the French, retreated south and east.

Napoleon III, Emperor of France, figured he'd set up a puppet regime in Mexico to oversee his new territory. He tapped an old friend, the Archduke Maximillian von Hapsburg of Austria, for the job. Maximillian and his wife, Carlota, arrived in Veracruz in 1864 to assume the title of Emperor and Empress of Mexico. To back them up, Napoleon III supplied 8,000 French Foreign Legionnaires to bolster whatever native army they created.

Back Like A Bad Penny

Maximillian's first decision about his Mexican forces caught everyone by surprise. In an astonishing move, he offered command of the Mexican Army to none other than Santa Anna! Eager for one more chance at power and glory, Santa Anna agreed to lead the newly-formed force. He had one condition, though: he wanted Maximillian to build him an army to retake Texas and avenge his humiliating 1836 and 1848 defeats. The Emperor agreed, but imposed a condition of his own—first Santa Anna would have to conquer California (later the Great Maze).

Lacking any alternative, Santa Anna agreed. Ever since then, he and his gaudily-clad Mexican soldiers have been trying to take the Maze, without much success. But Ol' One-Leg refuses to give up. From what I can tell, he sees this as his last opportunity to go down a hero and a conqueror, and he doesn't intend to miss it. If he's lucky, he may even get his missing leg back.

The Tombstone Epitaph's Guide to Mexico

1877 Edition   "Believe it or Else!"   Only 10¢

Mexican Standoff

The French Empire Of Mexico

The king of the mountain in Mexico right now is His Highness the Emperor Maximillian, an Austrian by birth, but Mexican by choice. He's ruled here for the past 14 years, though even he would have to admit that his rule has never extended throughout the entire country. His regime controls the central parts of Mexico—roughly everything north of a line drawn from Veracruz to Ixtapa, and south of a line from Tampico to Culiacán. He's eager to crush the rebels and bring the country under his banner, but that seems an unlikely outcome to me.

The Emperor

Maximillian himself is a tall, strong man with a black beard. I've heard women describe him as handsome. He's only 46 years old this year, and he's kept himself in pretty good shape. I understand he has a little military experience and can wield a saber well. He usually wears fancy European-style clothes or an ornate Mexican-style military uniform.

Maximillian started life as the Archduke of Austria. However, his brother, the Emperor Francis Joseph, made him (and Carlota) renounce all claims to the Austrian throne when he (Maximillian) accepted Napoleon III's offer, so there's no going back for him. He's got to do or die here in Mexico.

Most Mexicans hate Emperor Maximillian, and I can't say I blame them. After all, he's an invader, someone whom the French brought in to rule the country after they conquered it. But the ironic thing is, he's probably got Mexico's interests more at heart than anyone who's run the country this century. He takes his job seriously; he even bothered to learn Spanish, and uses it. He wants to improve education, and has tried to inspire a cultural revival by sponsoring scientific and artistic societies and encouraging new architectural styles. He's also attempted to give industry a kick in the pants to get it going, and even built a railroad between Mexico City and Veracruz. I'm told he's going to establish a university modelled after the Sorbonne in Paris. He even serves Mexican food at his table.

Of course, he is a European aristocrat, and he expects to be obeyed and toadied to "as an Emperor should be." That hasn't done much to make the people like him, and his laws enforcing the Church reforms of 20 years ago have alienated pretty much everyone. So, if he does send Santa Anna into Texas, the Confederacy can use that against him.

The Empress

Sitting at the Emperor's left-hand side is his Empress, Carlota (or "Charlotte" in her native tongue). By birth, she's the daughter of the king and queen of Belgium, and also a cousin of Great Britain's Queen Victoria. By all accounts, including mine, she's a pretty thing, and still only in her mid-30s. However, she has a haughty and condescending manner matching her husband's, which doesn't do much to endear her to anyone.

The Imperial couple live in Chapultepec Castle, a hundred-year-old building not far from Mexico City proper, rather than in the National Palace where most of the country's presidents have resided. Empress Carlota enjoys throwing parties, both at the Castle and at the Palace, and these events are the height of the Mexican social scene. I have been invited to several of them. They tend to be elaborate affairs, full of

71

18

The Tombstone Epitaph's Guide to Mexico

1877 Edition   "Believe it or Else!"   Only 10¢

exquisitely dressed people, where wearing, doing, and saying "just the right thing" is an absolute requirement. One slip and you're likely to become the butt of unpleasant jokes.

On a few occasions I managed to get near enough to the Empress to observe her closely. I expected a rather delicate and lighthearted woman devoted to all things social and fashionable, but that wasn't always what I found. She often seemed pensive, almost brooding, as if she had something heavy on her mind. If so, I never found out what it was. No one at the parties really seemed to notice.

The Emperor and Empress have no children. Shortly after arriving in Mexico, they adopted Agustín Iturbide, the grandson of Mexico's first emperor. However, they have not yet declared him the heir to their titles and position.

The Imperial Government

Emperor Maximillian reorganized his government a couple of years ago, probably in an effort to get rid of some deadwood and tighten his control over certain matters of state at the expense of Marshal Bazain. His frustration over his government's inability to deal with the rebels may also have played a part in the move.

The Imperial Council

The Emperor now receives advice from an "Imperial Council" made up of several ministers and other important officials. Most of these ministers run various governmental departments and agencies, but a few are simply "ministers without portfolio" who seem to be favorites of Maximillian's. The Imperial Council meets at the Emperor's behest to provide him with suggestions and information. It has no real power, though.

The "first among equals" in the Imperial Council seems to be Arturo Balthazar de Morelos, the Minister of Justice. He's responsible for the court system and *Policia Federal*—the Federal Police, which we know better as the "Rurales." More on them below. Balthazar's power results not only from his long friendship with, and support of, the Emperor, but his absolute control over the machinery of "justice" in

Maximillian's regime. I've heard rumors that the Emperor has decided that Balthazar's gotten *too* powerful and plans to throw him out of office. However, I think this is mostly wishful thinking on the part of the rumormongers.

Minister of Trade Guillaume d'Fleurisy, whom I believe the Emperor appointed at the behest of Napoleon III, is in charge of ensuring that Mexico pays its foreign debts to France and other countries. Between that and the Emperor's various projects, the Minister has to impose some pretty high taxes on the Mexican people. That certainly hasn't helped Maximillian win any popularity contests. In fact, I've heard Minister d'Fleurisy described as the most hated man in Mexico on more than one occasion.

Osvaldo Guttierez-Arias de Rovario heads the Ministry of War. Appointing a Mexican to this position was supposed to "prove" to the Mexican people that they ultimately controlled the army. Of course, that's not the case at all; Gutierrez-Arias has almost no power. He's just a figurehead for Marshal Bazain, who's forbidden by law from belonging to the Council but who nevertheless seems to attend all of its meetings.

The Emperor's close friend Jesús Flores y Maceda serves on the Council as Minister without Portfolio. I'm not quite sure exactly what the Emperor has him do, but he whispers in Maximillian's ear a lot. He misses plenty of Council meetings, so I suspect he's some kind of agent for the Emperor and Empress.

The rest of the ministers seem to me to be little more than career bureaucrats or political yes-men.

The Chamber Of Deputies

The closest thing the Empire of Mexico has to a legislature is the Chamber of Deputies. Each state, large or small, appoints two representatives to the Chamber for four-year terms. The Deputies don't really have any power to speak of, though. They petition the Emperor for favors or money for their states, and they can pass "laws" which the Emperor takes under advisement. But that's it; the Emperor doesn't have to listen to them if he doesn't want to.

Most of the Deputies are just longtime politicians appointed to the Chamber as payback from their state's governor, or perhaps because they know something about the

72

governor he'd rather they didn't. They're just in the job for the money and the perks, sort of like some of our representatives in the Confederate legislature. But I've noticed a couple who seem to be something more.

One of them's Miguel Vasquez-Trujillo, from Tamaulipas, a state bordering on Texas and the Gulf of Mexico. If I didn't know better I'd think he was really working for Benito Juárez. He's put forward several laws that sound a little like the sorts of laws Juárez was trying to pass while he was in power. The rest of the Deputies ignore him, for the most part, so the laws don't have a chance of making it to the Emperor, but he still keeps bringing them up.

73

Valentin Santanas-Orozco represents the tiny state of Aguascalientes, in the middle of the country. I find him noteworthy only because of his rabid support of Santa Anna's goal to retake Texas. Given his age, I wouldn't be surprised if he fought against the Texans in 1838 or 1848, or both. If he became popular, he would pose a definite danger to the Confederacy.

The Rurales

After the Texas Rangers helped defeat them so many times over the past thirty years or so, the Mexicans realized that the Rangers were too tough to tangle with. They decided that, as we Americans sometimes say, "if you can't beat 'em, join 'em," so they created a ranger group of their own. It's formally known as the *Policia Federal* (Federal Police), but everyone calls them *Rurales* ("Rurals") because they spend so much time out in the wilderness.

Like the Rangers, the Rurales have a lot of jobs. They enforce the Emperor's laws, and stay on the lookout for rustlers, road men, and banditos at all times. They fight Indians, specifically the Apaches who cause such trouble in the northern parts of the country (most other places the Indian and white populations have either interbred, or learned to live peaceably side by side). They also work as scouts and soldiers fighting Juárez's and Díaz's men.

One thing's for sure: they hate Texans. I've heard some of them talking about our good friends in the Lone Star State, and I gather a lot of them fought in the Mexican-American War.

They'd like nothing better than to help Santa Anna cross the Rio Grande and burn Houston and Austin to the ground. I believe their chances of success are small, but they either don't realize it, or won't believe it.

Although I don't think they're anywhere near as skilled as Rangers, or even Pinkertons, the Rurales would present a definite threat if the Confederate Army entered Mexico in response to Santa Anna's attacks. They know the land well, especially in the north, and the Mexican people seem to respect them.

State Government

Below the national government are the governments of the various Mexican states, which I named earlier in this article. Like the United States, Mexico has divided itself into many different states, each with its own governor, local legislature, and so forth. Most of the governing going on in Mexico takes place at the state level rather than the Imperial level. So does most of the corruption.

Each state has a governor whom it elects for terms varying from two years to six years. These elections are supposed to be open to all property-owning males, but somehow the candidate supported by the Emperor seems to win just about every one.

In states where Juárez or Díaz are strong, such as Sonora or Chihuahua up north or Oaxaca, Tabasco, and Chiapas down south, the governor has to perform a sort of balancing act. He has to remain loyal to the Emperor, the ruler of his country, but he doesn't dare express contempt for the rebels openly, since they'll drag him out of his house and shoot him if he does. He ends up trying to placate the rebels privately, while publicly professing his fealty to Maximillian. I don't envy the governors their jobs.

Most states also have their own local Chamber of Deputies, though they may call it something else. These groups actually have the power to pass laws, but the extent of their authority versus that of the governor varies from place to place. Local politics often gets much more heated and vicious than national politics—everyone knows who's in charge at the national level, but at the state level things are often very much undecided.

The Tombstone Epitaph's Guide to Mexico

The Mexican Military

The military has always been one of the most, if not *the* most, important institution in Mexico. Political change often starts with the military, where an ambitious officer like Santa Anna can spark a revolt which overthrows an unpopular or weak government.

Santa Anna has shown a willingness to turn on his supposed masters in the past, and he just might do it again if the situation looks favorable to him. Of course, if that happens, those who put him in power have no one to blame but themselves.

However, Emperor Maximillian is no fool. He's arranged things so that Santa Anna would have a difficult time pulling off any sort of military coup. There are in fact two Mexican armies—Santa Anna's Army of Northern Mexico, composed of both Mexican and French troops (and perhaps something more, as I discuss below), and the Emperor's Army of Southern Mexico, comprised mainly of Frenchmen, including the infamous French Foreign Legion. Overall about half of Mexico's soldiers are French, and the French have no loyalty to Santa Anna at all.

Military Command

Technically the commanders of the two armies, General Santa Anna and Marshal Bazain, have equal power. Each reports directly to the Emperor and commands his own men without consulting the other. However, the truth of the matter is that the Marshal, who has the Emperor's ear, is really in charge, and if necessary he can make Santa Anna follow his orders.

Marshal Bazain

Marshal Achille Bazain, Commander of His Imperial Majesty's Army of Southern Mexico, is one of Napoleon III's oldest and dearest friends and, at one time, was one of his most trusted advisors. I suspect that he still is, and that Napoleon III sent him to Mexico with Maximillian so he could keep an eye on Napoleon III's pet archduke.

Bazain is a crusty old bird who's seen well over a dozen military campaigns during his career. He doesn't tolerate any breaking of discipline or lack of courage on the part of his men, and has no qualms about handing out

A group of *rurales* on patrol.

The Tombstone Epitaph's Guide to Mexico

1877 Edition   "Believe it or Else!"   Only 10¢

severe punishments for any infractions. He always goes before his men dressed in his formal uniform, without a button out of place or a single smear of dirt to mar his appearance.

He may look like something of a fop, but no one can deny that he's an extremely skilled tactician. I've heard stories about some of his campaigns back home and how he took an outnumbered force in a poor tactical position and turned the entire battle around with just a few brilliant maneuvers. As good as Santa Anna is, I'll bet that if they went *mano a mano*, Marshal Bazain could outfox him. However, Santa Anna has one thing Bazain never will: the love of the Mexican people. From what I can tell, no one in Mexico besides the Emperor and the soldiers likes the Marshal. The Mexicans remember all too well how he led the French troops that conquered the country and gave no quarter to his opponents. Plenty of Mexicans would gladly slit his throat for a peso or two. That's why he has two well-trained bodyguards—one French, one Indian—with him wherever he goes.

Marshal Achille Bazain.

Colonel Castelnau

Marshal Bazain's second in command is Colonel Philippe Castelnau. You couldn't ask for two men who are more unlike each other than these two. Castelnau seems to have gotten his job because he knew someone important, not because he can lead men in battle. He likes all the fancy uniforms, parades, dress balls, and things like that—anything that helps him impress women or lets him enjoy himself—but I've never actually seen him out in the field commanding troops. I think his idea of soldiering is to stay back at headquarters and issue orders to his officers by messenger. The men call him "the Little Bluebird" behind his back, and the "ladies" who always seem to follow in the wake of his party when he does go into the field are "bluebirds."

75

Castelnau's good for one thing, though—the diplomatic functions where Marshal Bazain's blunt manner just tends to aggravate and anger people. Castelnau is nothing if not the accomplished courtier and negotiator, so he's the one sent to meet with state governors, visiting officials, and others whom the Marshal would offend.

Corporal Willette

Marshal Bazain's aide-de-camp is a man named Willette. I don't know what his first name is, and no one else seems to, either. He used to be a Legionnaire, but somehow he impressed Bazain and was made his aide. From what I've heard, Corporal Willette is the one who keeps the Marshal and his office functioning so efficiently. He's a quiet and sober man whom the soldiers call "the Padre" because he looks just like a Mexican friar.

75

Military Structure

The Mexican Army is a sort of tangle. To begin with, it includes two different types of soldiers: French and Mexican. About half of the country's 60,000 troops are Frenchmen, including 8,000 Legionnaires. Most of them are stationed in or around Mexico City, and commanded directly by Marshal Bazain and Col.

Castelnau. Most of the French soldiers are veterans who have served here for years. They're tough, professional soldiers who would give the Confederate Army quite a scrap if push came to shove between Mexico and the Confederacy.

The other half of the army includes the "native" soldiers, as the French call them—the Mexicans. Some of them are up with Santa Anna fighting in California, while the rest fight the rebels or man posts elsewhere in the country. They look mighty impressive, with their fancy uniforms and well-polished rifles and swords, but I don't know how good they are in a fight. The squabbles up in California have shown they can hold their own, at least, but I'm not so sure Santa Anna can count on them for the long haul of the large-scale invasion he seems to be planning. A lot of them are veterans—they fought in the wars against the French 15 years ago, and they've been fighting rebels and Californians since then, so they won't turn tail and run the first time you come up against them. They're also used to marching and fighting in the Mexican desert, something that the French soldiers still haven't gotten accustomed to.

Emperor Maximillian seems to want to merge the two armies more—to form joint Mexican and French units—but that probably won't happen soon. For one thing, most of the French soldiers don't speak Spanish, and the Mexicans *je ne parle pas Francais*, so getting them to work together would take some effort. More importantly, Marshal Bazain and General Santa Anna don't seem too keen on the idea. While Maximillian is something of an idealist who wants to build a firm foundation for what he thinks is going to be an imperial dynasty, the military commanders just want men who are loyal to them and fight well.

Units

French or Mexican, the armies of the Empire of Mexico are organized in pretty much the same fashion. Each one has several brigades with maybe 5,000-10,000 men in each; brigades are commanded by brigadier generals. Each brigade contains two or more battalions of 2,000-4,000 men apiece commanded by a colonel. Battalions have several 500-800 man regiments, with each regiment containing three to seven companies. Majors or captains command regiments, and captains command companies. Within each company are several platoons (20-40 men each) commanded by a lieutenant, or sometimes a sergeant. Regiments and brigades seem to form the basic units within the army; most of the time soldiers think of themselves as belonging to one of them, rather than to a battalion.

The French Foreign Legion

Without a doubt, the most competent military unit in Mexico, and the most feared, is *La Legion Etrangere*—the French Foreign Legion. Composed of hard-bitten veteran troops who seem to emerge victorious even when greatly outnumbered, the Legion has established a reputation for skill and ferocity which few armies can match.

Right now there are about 8,000 Legionnaires in Mexico, and I find every one of them frightening. Most are out in the field—helping Santa Anna, or going after rebels, or guarding the French territory between Mexico City and Veracruz. They're not the sort of soldiers who like to sit around camps near the capital for months at a time—they'd rather be busting skulls than spit-polishing their boots.

Men Without A Country

Although many of them adopt a French name when the join the Legion, Legionnaires aren't Frenchmen originally. Instead, as the group's name implies, it only takes non-Frenchmen. The Legion includes soldiers from most of the civilized nations on Earth—everywhere from Spain to **76** Russia. The Legion doesn't care what a man did before he came to it; as long as he's of sound mind and body, they'll sign him up. The result is an army filled with murderers, thieves, convicts given a choice of prison or enlistment, men on the run, soldiers who were busted out of other armies for insubordination, brokenhearted fools, and others with nothing to lose. Men who join the Legion have all sorts of experience—anything from a student or artist, to blacksmiths, to shipwrights. You name it, the Legion's got someone who can do it. They become French, as they say, not by birth, but by the blood they shed.

The Tombstone Epitaph's Guide to Mexico

The Legionaire's valiant stant at Limarón.

Since the French have no real connection to the Legion, they use it to do all the dirty work they don't want their sons and brothers to do. The Legion's sent all over the world, to the worst hell-holes and battlefields men have ever created, to fight and die for a country which isn't even theirs. It's said the Legion never surrenders, no matter how bad the odds against it.

Camarón's a little village between Veracruz and Mexico City which was destroyed during the fighting between the French and Mexicans back when the Frenchies took over the country. The 3rd Company of the 1st Battalion of the Legion was given the job of getting a wagonload of French gold from the coast to Mexico City to pay the soldiers there. Along the way they were attacked by Mexicans, and took refuge in the ruins of Camarón. About 50 Legionnaires held out there for nine hours against 2,000 Mexicans. Their commander, Captain Jean Danjou, refused to surrender. After he was killed, the men who stepped up to take his place refused to surrender, too, and died in their turn. The Legion fought right down to the last man before they let the Mexicans get their hands on that gold. Only six of them, none unwounded, survived the ordeal. Such is the stuff of which Legionnaires are made.

Legion Training

The Legion's headquarters is located in the deserts of Algeria. New recruits are sent there for weeks of hard physical labor and brutal military training. Those who survive the process—and not all recruits do by any means—become the toughest soldiers in the world. They certainly don't flinch at marching through the Mexican heat, and they're as good at desert fighting as any Apache.

The Legion contains almost nothing but infantry. There are a few mounted units, and occasionally they'll form an artillery company when they have the hardware available, but the typical Legionnaire is a dog soldier who's used to marching for miles across the worst sort of terrain.

To say that the Legion disciplines its soldiers harshly is an understatement. Commanders run their units with an iron grip, and any sort of insubordination or disobedience will get a soldier thrown into a military jail to roast in the heat. Repeated offenses merit manual labor in chains in the Algerian or Mexican sun. Anything worse than simple infractions may just get the offending Legionnaire shot by a firing squad.

94

The Legion's particularly determined to capture anyone who deserts from its ranks. Since it arrived in Mexico, it's lost more than a few soldiers to America, since a lot of men would rather swim the Rio Grande and make their way Back East to try to build better lives for themselves in the Confederacy or the Union. The Legion has no qualms about pursuing deserters and dragging them all the way back to Mexico to face court-martial and execution.

I heard a story from a Legionnaire I bought some *cerveza* for in a village not far from Mexico City about a soldier who deserted only a couple of years after the Frenchies arrived in Mexico. They way this guy told it, the deserter fled north to El Paso, and from there went on to St. Louis, where he got a job with one of the railroads and married a local girl. Everything went fine for ten years, but then the Legion got word somehow about the deserter's whereabouts. A squad of disguised Legionnaires made their way to St. Louis, where they found the man, slapped him in chains, and brought him all the way back to Mexico City. The next day he was tried, shot, and tossed outside the city for the coyotes.

I'm not so sure I believe this story—it sounds a little farfetched for soldiers, even disguised ones, to be able to kidnap someone and get him out of the Confederacy without the Texas Rangers finding out about it. But I suppose it's possible. Legionnaires are typically equipped with chassepot rifles, a highly accurate single-shot longarm. Many also pick up discarded Mexican or American pistols of various kinds. The high firepower of repeaters like the Winchester make these prized finds for the Legionnaires.

Command

The Legion has ten battalions in Mexico, each with at least three or four companies in it. A major commands each battalion, and captains lead the companies. The overall commander of the Legion in Mexico is Colonel Pierre Jeanningros, who usually stays at the 6th Battalion's command post near Veracruz. Jeanningros has been in Mexico with the Legion from day one, and before that he fought in Algeria and plenty of other godforsaken places around the world.

Legion companies and squads are usually garrisoned at small fortresses they built themselves after the French conquered Mexico. In the north they tend to be wood and adobe; in the east and south they're all wood, or sometimes even stone. Important cities or areas like Mexico City, Veracruz, and Guadalajara have larger, better-manned forts. I'll discuss some of the forts in the next section of my report, especially the ones on our Mexican border which have caused us so much trouble.

Santa Anna's Army

The Legion would be a tough opponent for the Confederate army, but right now it's Santa Anna and his army which poses the biggest threat to the Confederacy. Although I'm sure that readers of the *Epitaph* have heard about the events in California from this newspaper and other sources, I decided I should include everything I've managed to learn in this article in case any of it's new to you.

General Santa Anna

My earlier recitation of recent Mexican history explored the ups and downs of Santa Anna's background, so I won't repeat that information here. Suffice it to say that he poses an extreme danger to the Confederacy—particularly now that he's got someone with money backing him.

Santa Anna himself is a tall, regal-looking fellow with white skin and an elegant black moustache. His noble heritage shines through in his every look and movement. He wears a fancy Mexican army uniform, but since he's the sort of commander who likes to lead from the field, it's often a little rumpled and dirty. However, rumpled or not, it's impossible to overlook the aura of command which surrounds him. He's been a leader of nations and men for forty years, and it shows. He knows how to inspire, give orders, lead by example, and cut someone down to size with a well-timed comment.

Thanks to all the time he's spent leading armies, Santa Anna is a dangerous opponent to face in any kind of battle. I haven't fought him, of course, not being a military man myself, but I'm told that other than the wily Marshal Bazain, there's no one south of the Rio

76

Tequila and hot lead, 2 Mexican specialties.

Grande who can even come close to matching his tactical and strategic skills. He's also said to be a crack shot with pistol or rifle, a fencer good enough to put a graduate of Heidelberg to shame, and a skilled rider. Of course, that peg leg of his slows him down a little bit, but they say he's gotten used to it by now.

Forty years of experience at the forefront of Mexican politics has given Santa Anna plenty of other skills to complement his martial ones. He's a smooth talker, diplomat, and politician who's managed to worm his way back into power again and again despite humiliating defeats and countless enemies. He knows everyone in Mexico who holds any kind of power, and most of them owe him favors. He can play court politics, too; it's no mistake that he's the only Mexican holding a position of real power in Maximillian's regime.

Santa Anna's real ambition—invading and conquering Texas—isn't exactly a secret. That's why he took the job from the Emperor in the first place, for the chance to get an army at his back and take it across the Rio Grande. If he

tries it, the Texans will no doubt make him run back to Mexico City so fast he won't know what hit him.

I've also heard that Santa Anna would like to get his stolen artificial leg back. I have no idea why he wants it so badly, but he intends to get his hands on it.

78

Santa Anna's Advisors

Santa Anna's a mighty clever fellow, but he's smart enough to know that he's got so much going on that he needs good folks to help him out. Accordingly, he travels with an entourage of handpicked assistants.

His second in command, a trusted friend of long standing, is Brigadier General Emiliano Urabazo de Salgado y Landrón. The two of them went to the Mexican military academy together and came up through the ranks at the same time. General Landrón lacks Santa Anna's political and diplomatic skills, but possesses a measure of tactical and military genius almost equal to that of his commander. When Santa Anna gets caught up in his dreams of conquest and glory, Landrón is there to make sure that the army continues to run smoothly towards those goals.

Santa Anna's other chief advisor is a relative newcomer, and a strange one at that. He's an old Indian shaman named Xitlan. I haven't been able to find out much about him, not even his tribe, though I'd guess from his name and appearance that he's Zapotec.

I've heard the two of them met during Santa Anna's exile on Jamaica, but I have no proof of that. I also have no idea why Santa Anna would turn to an Indian shaman for any sort of military advice. Xitlan doesn't even seem to come out of his tent much during the day. But for all I know, he's got some way of reading the General's horoscope that Santa Anna thinks works.

99

The Army Of Northern Mexico

Santa Anna's main army is composed of both Mexicans and Frenchmen, though the Mexicans dominate by about two to one. The army contains about 15,000 soldiers at present, organized into two brigades.

So far they haven't had much luck in California, though I think that's about to change. Initially Santa Anna only had about 5,000 *soldados* under his command. Although that still gave him the largest military force in the Great Maze region, the chaotic conditions there prevented him from being able to bring his forces to bear. As a result, he lost battles at Palo Alto, Resaca de la Palma, Monterrey, and Buena Vista to either the Union or our boys in grey that he really ought to have won.

But it seems as though he's finally decided to stop pussyfooting around. Reinforced with enough soldiers to more than double the size of his army, including a large number of Legionnaires, he seems to be getting ready for a real push into the Maze, as discussed further below. I don't think he's going to stop until he's brought the Maze firmly under Maximillian's thumb and he can turn his attention to the Lone Star State.

The Army Of The Night

However, that's not Santa Anna's only army. He's got another one—one that only marches and fights at night. You've probably heard rumors of this *Ejército De Los Muertos*, an army of the undead—and I'm here to tell you that those rumors may be true.

While in northern Mexico, I ran across the trail of a large column of troops. I was intrigued as to what they were up to, so I trailed behind at a discreet distance. The column marched all through the night and made camp just as the first light of dawn began to break.

The cover around the camp was sparse, and they had sentries posted, so I wasn't able to get too close. However, what little I was able to see from my vantage point was disturbing. The troops' uniforms were dirty and disheveled; unusual for Mexican troops who normally take peacock-like pride in their appearance. Those who were not standing a post did nothing. They didn't cook, set up tents, or play cards—they simply sat motionless in the baking sun while flies gathered around the camp in the thousands.

I was spotted before I could get a closer look, and I was forced to beat a hasty retreat into the desert. The short glimpse I got, though, made me fear for the future.

79

The Mexican Navy

Mexico has a navy to go with its army, of course—paid for with French francs. Right now just about the entire fleet is in or near the Great Maze, trying to support Santa Anna's army from the sea. Unfortunately, I know little or nothing about the navy, so I cannot report on it further.

The *Juaristas*

Of course, Maximillian and Carlota aren't the only powers in Mexico. A couple of other folks have been trying to kick them out and take power for themselves for the past dozen years or more. The first, and most popular, of these is the former president of the country, Benito Juárez.

Benito Juarez

A Zapotec Indian, Benito Juárez grew up an orphan in the southern state of Oaxaca. A patron sponsored him to the seminary; afterward, he studied law and got into politics. Before long he got elected to the governorship of Oaxaca. But that was only the start.

Thanks to his ideas about governmental reform, Juárez was exiled by Santa Anna. He soon got involved in the Ayutla revolution, serving as secretary to one of its leaders. When his boss became president of the country, he was appointed Minister of Justice. The next year, 1855, he was elected president himself. That gave him the opportunity to sponsor all kinds of reform laws—not all of which proved popular with the rich. That led to the War of the Reform, which I mentioned earlier, and eventually to the French conquest of Mexico. When the French approached Mexico City in 1862, Juárez fled to the northwestern part of Mexico along with his supporters and many soldiers.

80

The People's Rebel

Knowing they didn't have a prayer of defeating the well-trained French in an outright battle, Juárez and his followers took their cue from the Apaches and began living the life of the outlaw. Instead of fighting battles, they lived off the land and conducted raids and ambushes.

That was 15 years ago, and they're still at it. Their greatest triumph to date was the 1872 ambush and massacre of nearly a hundred Legionnaires near Santa Isabella. Thanks to the fact Juárez enjoys enormous popular support— Mexicans everywhere, even some of the wealthy who used to compare him to the Antichrist, want to see him succeed and return to the presidency—he and his forces have managed to stay one step ahead of the French and Mexican Army patrols sent after them.

The reason Mexicans like Juárez is simple: he's a good man. Even though his reforms go a little far for some folks, at heart I think all he really wants is a Mexico run by Mexicans where everyone gets treated fairly. He's not interested in creating an empire, or recovering lands lost in past wars, or anything like that—he just wants good, honest government. I doubt he's ever going to get it, but that's why he's the people's hero.

Juaristas with the *Rurales* in pursuit.

Juarez's Forces

Compared to Santa Anna's army, or even Díaz's, the *Juaristas*, as they're called, are a pretty ragtag bunch. I'd estimate there's no more than two or three thousand of them, at best, and they never gather in the same place at the same time. They don't have uniforms or standard equipment; they make do with whatever clothes, guns, and food they can recover from their opponents, steal, or buy from Mexicans loyal to them. As a result, they've got a mix of everything from chassepots, to Winchesters, to cap-and-ball rifles which were new half a century ago. Just getting enough ammunition and food to keep the Juaristas going is a major problem for Juárez, but somehow he's kept them fighting and riding for over a dozen years.

Ranking below Juárez are several trusted men referred to as "captains." They, in turn, give orders to lieutenants, sergeants, and so on, but the truth is the group is more a large band of raiders than a real military force. They're disciplined—they have to be, to devote themselves to such a hopeless cause for so long—but it's not the crisp military sort of discipline you'll see among Santa Anna's men.

Hit 'Em Fast, Hit 'Em Hard

Bands of Juaristas usually number no more than a hundred, at most, and 20-30 is more like it in most cases. Since they can't stand up to the Legion or the regular Mexican Army in a battle, they settle for hit-and-run tactics copied from the Apaches. They ride in quick, grab what they need or shoot at whichever soldiers are too slow to get behind cover, and then get the hell away. Once they make it back into the deserts, hills, and *arroyos*, not even the Legion has much hope of finding them. Even if they did find them, they'd be so well holed up that it would take a thousand men just to dig them out.

Sometimes, though, several groups of Juaristas will get together to take on a big target, like a military convoy taking weapons and supplies to Santa Anna, or a detachment of Legionnaires who've strayed too far from safety. All those *campesinos* and other people who look up to Juárez pass his men information about such things. The Juaristas have to be careful—sometimes spies plant decoy stories to lure them out into the open so the Legion can fight them—but when they sense they're on to something big, they take the chance.

Territory

Juárez and his forces stick to the northern part of the country, mostly along the west coast. They control most of the state of Sinaloa, and substantial parts of Sonora, Durango, and Chihuahua. Santa Anna's supply caravans go through these areas only under heavy guard.

Sometimes the Juaristas venture as far west as Coahuila, but they don't go further than that—they're afraid of the Legion's 2nd Battalion, which Marshal Bazain has headquartered in Monterrey. Similarly, they don't usually go south of Durango or Zacatecas (if they do, they usually hug the coast, where they have strong support). However, they have friends and supporters all over Mexico, so if they need to send a small band of fighters somewhere for an important mission, they can do it without attracting any attention.

The *Porfiriatistas*

The Juaristas' opposite number, in more ways than one, are the followers of Porfirio Díaz—the *Porfiriatistas*. They occupy a lot of territory down south.

Porfirio Diaz

Díaz himself has been around Mexican politics pretty much as long as Juárez. He's a *mestizo* who was born in Oaxaca way back in 1830. Like Juárez, he first studied in the seminary, then left it to attend law school. However, unlike the Juarista leader he never completed his legal training, instead opting for a military career. During the initial French invasion he led the troops which repelled the French attack at Puebla, earning him the Frenchmen's undying hatred. When the French brought in reinforcements and Juárez abandoned Mexico City, Díaz took his forces south, into his homeland and the Yucatán Peninsula, where

he knew the land better than the Frenchmen ever could or would. Since then he's been holding out down there, waiting for the opportunity to strike a telling blow at the French. They call him "the Phantom General" because of the way he and his forces fade away into the wilderness whenever they pursue him.

Although many people regard him as a hero, if you ask me, Díaz is nothing but trouble in the long run. He's not the sort of man Juárez is; he's cold, callous, cruel, and calculating. All he thinks about is himself and his quest for control of Mexico. He's not interested in returning Juárez or anyone else to power.

Anyone who doesn't do what Díaz wants takes a big risk. Back during the initial campaign against the French, he once had an entire company of men shot for disobeying his orders, and I have no doubt he's left a few of his Porfiriatistas in unmarked graves down south when they questioned his commands. Díaz has a policy of *pan o palo*—"bread or the stick." In other words, do what he wants, and you'll be rewarded; go against his wishes and he'll have you beaten.

Diaz's Forces

Díaz controls three or four thousand men, at best guess. Like the Juaristas, he tends to keep them split up into smaller groups so that it's easier to keep them supplied and out of the eyes of the French. However, Díaz expects absolute military discipline from his men. He usually gets it, too, since his men are mostly former Mexican soldiers, and they know he's likely to have them shot if they don't do as they're told.

If there's anyone in the Porfiriatista army who's as mean as Díaz himself, it's probably his second in command, Rafael Velasco-Burgos. He's about the ugliest man I've ever seen—he's got pockmarked skin, black teeth, and only one eye (he lost the other to a French bullet)—and his mind is even uglier. If anything, the men are more scared of him than of Díaz, since Velasco-Burgos sometimes lashes out at them for no good reason. At least Díaz has the sense to treat his men reasonably well if they do their jobs right.

So, why do the soldiers stay around if they're treated so badly? Well, in a word, power. They're placing their bets on Díaz to come into

82

The Tombstone Epitaph's Guide to Mexico

1877 Edition   "Believe it or Else!"   Only 10¢

control of Mexico sooner or later. When he does, they expect to reap the rewards for their faithful service—money, government jobs, the whole shebang. Kind of makes the whole nasty business worth it, doesn't it?

Territory

The Porfiriatistas have control, more or less, of most of the southern part of the country—places like Oaxaca, Chiapas, Tabasco, Campeche, and the rest of the Yucatán Peninsula. Maximillian and the French pretend that they run things there, but their power only extends as far as their hands (or bullets) reach. Once they march away from an area, the Porfiriatistas take control again.

Díaz doesn't have the sort of popular support and help that Juárez gets, but that doesn't matter to him and his men. If they need something—cattle, grain, or a place to say, for example—they just ride to the nearest village or farm and take it. Whether the peasants want to give it to them

This mission has fallen on hard times.

doesn't even cross their minds. The people don't like it, but they tolerate it, not only because he and his men will kill them if they protest, but because when it comes down to it, they'd rather see him in charge than the French.

Other Folks

Maximillian, Juárez, and Díaz aren't the only folks to consider if you come down here to Mexico. There are a few other things to take into account. If you don't watch your step, you may run afoul of them.

The Catholic Church

Ever since the Spaniards pacified the Aztecs and other Indian tribes, Mexico has been a Roman Catholic country. It seems like every village, no matter how small, has its little adobe church, and the cathedrals in places like Mexico City are the equal of anything you'll see over in Europe. In most villages and towns the most influential people you'll find are the local priests and friars.

In fact, not so long ago the Church owned roughly half of the entire country of Mexico. Juárez's reforms took that land away from it, to the shock and indignation of many not-so-devout priests who'd gotten fat and happy on Church riches.

Many churchmen, including Antonio Pelagio Labastida, Archbishop of Mexico, supported Maximillian for this reason. They figured that Maximillian, a Catholic who consulted Pope Pius IX before taking the job of emperor, would give them back their land and power. Archbishop Labastida even presided over some of the welcoming ceremonies for the new Emperor and Empress.

Unfortunately for the Church, Maximillian hasn't done anything to restore their lands. So, now you've got three types of priests out there: apologists for the Imperial regime, who keep hoping Maximillian will favor them; priests who've decided Maximillian isn't the friend of the Church they thought he was, and that he should be condemned (I understand the Pope likes this

83

The Tombstone Epitaph's Guide to Mexico

1877 Edition   "Believe it or Else!"   Only 10¢

idea); and a silent minority who thinks the Church didn't really need all those lands anyway (these gents usually favor Juárez). You'd be wise to determine which camp the local *padre* falls into before you start talking politics with him; given his prominence in the town, if you cause trouble for him, he'll cause difficulties for you in return. Despite its occasional abuses, the campesinos still hold the church in high regard.

The *Campesinos*

Campesino is a Spanish word meaning "countrysideman"—in other words, farmers and peasants. Most of the people of Mexico fall into this class. They grow corn and chilis, raise pigs and goats, all that kind of thing. It's not a very pleasant or rewarding life, but they make do with what they've got.

The campesinos don't wield a whole lot of raw political power—they don't even get to vote for anyone, except maybe the local governor if they're lucky—but they're *everywhere*. If you get them angry or scared enough, they'll come after you in a pitchfork-and-scythe-wielding mob (trust me, I know whereof I speak). With all the unusual happenings over the past fourteen years, they've developed sharp eyes for things that are out of place and need to be put down hard.

Campesinos know which way the wind's blowing, so they shut up and keep their eyes pointed groundward whenever French troops or the Porfiriatistas come around. But most of them support Juárez, and I imagine that if the Confederacy decided to help Benito get rid of the French, they'd be a big asset.

Indians

Although the Aztecs are long gone, having been slaughtered or interbred into the population, Mexico still has a pretty substantial population of what I think of as "civilized" Indian tribes. For the most part, these Indians have adopted an agricultural life-style, and even accepted the Catholic Church (though their rituals and ceremonies seem to blend in a lot of the old Indian religions, too—and I suspect they discard papal trappings entirely on some occasions).

Down in the Valley of Oaxaca, near the old ruins at Monte Albán, you'll find plenty of Zapotecs—Benito Juárez's people. They're mainly farmers and herders. I don't think most of them know or care much about what their ancestors did.

Cheek by jowl with the Zapotecs are the Mixtecs, the "cloud people" of northern and western Oaxaca. Like their forebears, they're hunters, and sometimes farmers as well. A few of them have maintained their peoples' ancient traditions of gold working. They create some beautiful jewelry that even the Europeans find attractive.

Large parts of the Yucatán are still settled by pure-blooded Maya Indians. They farm lands right next to the ruins of the Maya empires of a thousand years ago. They seem to have adopted the Catholic Church much less than the other civilized tribes.

The biggest *uncivilized* tribe in Mexico is probably the Apaches. They live in the northern part of the country, which allows them to raid south into the more settled parts of Mexico or north into the Confederacy. Many *Epitaph* readers have also read a report from an Indian named Charley Bull that describes the Apaches (among others). The Apaches of northern Mexico aren't as elusive as Geronimo and his Chiricahuas, but they are still a large thorn in the side of the Rurales.

Actin' Neighborly

Mexico's in such a mess right now, no one there is paying a whole lot of attention to foreign relations. But here's where things stand, as near as I can tell.

The Confederacy

Mexico doesn't get along with the fine folk of the Confederacy very well. Relations are cordial on the face of things, but just beneath the surface there's a lot of ill will. Santa Anna's troops have battled ours out in the Great Maze, and our navies have clashed there more than once. The biggest bone of contention, of course, is Texas (and to a lesser extent all the other

The Tombstone Epitaph's Guide to Mexico

1877 Edition   "Believe it or Else!"   Only 10¢

land Mexico lost to the U.S. a few decades ago). Thanks to their long history of conflict and disputes, Mexicans hate Texans, and the feeling's mutual. They particularly don't like the Rangers; they remember how Rangers helped get rid of them and make Texas an independent country, and they've never forgiven them for this "mistreatment." Santa Anna isn't alone in wanting to invade the Lone Star State and take it back. But I don't believe he's a match for the fine men of Texas.

The Union

Mexico's relations with the United States aren't much better. Santa Anna's forces have fought Union troops in California, though not as often or as hard as he's fought ours. Most Mexican-US clashes have been of the naval variety. Mexicans still rankle over losing all that territory in the Mexican-American War, and they'd really like it back. But for now they seem willing to let that matter wait until they take over Texas.

A Mexican *Bandito* looks tough for the camera.

California Or Bust?

Of course, the most likely point of contention between Santa Anna and either the Confederacy or the Union, at least initially, is the Great Maze. Santa Anna has fought there in the past, and been defeated, but any clever observer could tell you that he was hampered by long supply lines and his lack of full financial or military support from his French masters.

That seems to have changed. For the past several months, Santa Anna's been camped out on the Baja California peninsula. If you look at your map, on the west coast of Mexico you'll see a long peninsula pointing south like a finger. That's Baja California. It's a fine and pleasant land which combines the best of Mexico's sunshine and good weather with cool sea breezes. It's mostly uninhabited; the city of Tijuana, once on the northern border, tumbled right into the ocean along with San Diego when the Great Maze was created. Plenty of salvagers, scavengers, prospectors, and pirates live there now, making a living sifting through the ruins, mining ghost rock, or preying on their fellow man. The biggest city in the region now is Mexicali, also on the northern border but further east.

As of the time I write this report, Santa Anna remains camped out in Baja only a few dozen miles south of Mexicali. He's been reinforced by over 10,000 troops sent up from Mexico City. No one is entirely sure exactly what his plans are, but a full-scale invasion of California seems inevitable. The best guess seems to be that he'd head up the Ghost Trail through the Mojave, one slow, burning mile at a time, slowing ghost rock shipments to Arizona and Texas down to a trickle. He'd take the cities and towns one at a time, since none of them could stand against him. Kwan Province would probably put up a fight and be crushed —Santa Anna wouldn't even need to use his zombie army.

But then he'd come up against Lost Angels. Many *Epitaph* readers are no doubt better informed than I, but it's my understanding that Rev. Grimme and his flock are arming themselves and preparing to meet any Mexican invaders hammer and tongs. It sounds ridiculous to me—a bunch of untrained worshippers taking on either of Santa

Anna's armies seems tantamount to suicide—but I've seen stranger things in the Weird West, and faith in God can be a powerful motivator. Ironically enough, I think the two forces are most likely to meet near a little town called Riverside on the Santa Anna River.

If Grimme's forces can't slow Santa Anna down long enough for Confederate (and perhaps Union) forces to find a way to turn back his invasion for good, California's in big trouble. There's pretty much no force between Lost Angels and Shan Fan right now that can stand up to the Mexican army (living *or* dead). Even with time to prepare, the odds of resisting a force the size of Santa Anna's are pretty damn slim.

Is There Someone Else Out There?

As Mr. O'Malley could tell you, Good Reader, I'm not one who's given to idle speculation. But I get the feeling that there's something going on beneath the surface here in Mexico. As I walk around Mexico City, I sense an undercurrent of some kind. It could be the restless dead—heaven knows enough people have been slaughtered in this city over the past 350 years—but it doesn't feel quite like that. When I talk to the people out in the countryside, I get the impression they're keeping something to themselves. That wouldn't surprise me, since shooting their mouths off usually gets them shot, either by the French or Díaz, but it's still odd.

Somehow, I get the feeling this relates to the Indians. Maybe even, through some process spawned of whatever birthed the weirdness which has infected the West, the Aztecs, which is why I spent so much time and paper talking about them earlier in this report. Lately I've been seeing more Indians in the city, doing things they don't normally do—like Xitlan advising Santa Anna. It makes little sense to me, but perhaps by the next time Mr. O'Malley asks me to write for his publication, I—or one of you, Good Readers—will have learned more. Until then, I'll keep my eyes and ears open. I just hope the truth comes out soon.

Travel Guide

Just so any travelers who come down here don't get lost, here's a brief guide to some of the typical places and people they might encounter. Refer back to the first section of my report if you need information on the basic geography of the country.

Village Life

Although my report discusses several cities below, most Mexicans are men of the countryside, not of the city. They live in villages (or sometimes small towns) and farm the surrounding countryside.

Most of these villages look very much the same, as if God made them from the same mold and simply set them down on the Earth. The buildings are made of adobe (a glorified form of dried mud) and wood. Glass is a rarity; most windows are protected by curtains or wooden shutters. But neither method serves to keep out the omnipresent dust. Except in the southern parts of the country, where they see rain frequently enough, Mexico's a dusty, dirty country. You'll see the dust everywhere, from the clothing and uniforms of the people, to the outsides and interiors of buildings, to inside your own saddlebag. Be sure to wear a handkerchief over your mouth and nose when you ride.

The village's two most prominent buildings are the village church and the *cantina* (saloon). I described the churches and village priests, who wield enormous influence, earlier in this report. Cantinas are discussed a bit below. Together church and saloon form the major cultural institutions. Most villages have few, if any, other shops, and the ones they do have sell the basics: food, horse-shoeing, that sort of thing. Don't plan to tour the Mexican countryside to shop.

Villagers are mostly farmers. They have a few acres, maybe a burro or horse, and perhaps some cattle, pigs, goats, or sheep. They barely manage to scrape a living from the ground through backbreaking hard labor by working from before sunrise until after sunset. They usually don't have any defense against the bandits and soldiers who prey upon them.

La Nacion y la Gente

The Border

The Confederacy's got a big border with Mexico—almost two thousand miles' worth of it. The border runs all the way from the Gulf Coast to the Pacific Ocean.

Crossing The Border

For the most part, it's not too hard to get across the border. People—including Apaches—go back and forth across it all the time. Most of it isn't patrolled or protected at all; the Confederacy simply doesn't have the forces to spare. Mexicans, Confederates, Apaches, Legionnaires, and anyone else who wants to can cross more or less at his leisure.

Even the Rio Grande doesn't pose much of an obstacle, except near the sea. Back in the desert areas, it's a pretty shallow river in most places, fairly easy to wade or ride across if you watch your step. If you'd rather not go to that trouble, many places have ferries.

Of course, there are a few dangers to avoid. Bandit gangs and Apache raiders are one such problem—they'll kill most travelers and strip the corpses bare if they get the chance. Other dangers, such as Legionnaires or strange Western creatures, are discussed below.

Rustlers

Among other things, this situation causes a lot of cattle and horse rustling. Banditos from Mexico cross the border into the Confederacy to lift some enterprising cattleman's choicest beeves, or maybe to take a string of ponies. Once they get back to their own side of the border, the odds of that cattleman, or a posse, or even a Texas Ranger finding them on their home ground are slim. Before you know it those steers will be steaks on the plates of the well-to-do in Monterrey and Mexico City. And it works in reverse, too—rustlers from our side, like that Cowboy gang over in Tombstone, can snatch some Mexican cattle and have them back over the border before they can moo. Unfortunately I don't think there's any way to stop this from happening unless the Confederates patrolled the entire border.

Vaqueros And Haciendas

One of the reasons there's all this rustling going on is that the Mexicans use their border country to raise cattle, just like we do. They've got a type of cowboy called a *vaquero* to watch over them. Vaqueros aren't much different from our kind of cowboys; it's more a matter of style and attitude. Vaqueros are even crazier about spending their money on fancy things and liquor than the American cowboy. For example, their pants often have rows of silver decorations made from coins down the outside edges, and their hats sometimes have fancy gold-thread embroidery and other embellishments. One time I saw a vaquero riding an old nag—with a two thousand dollar gold-and-silver-inlaid saddle! Only in Mexico.

Vaqueros typically work on *haciendas*. That's a Spanish term meaning a big landed estate—sort of like a cross between a Back East plantation and a traditional western ranch. Men who work on them, including vaqueros, are generally known as *rancheros*. Hacienda also refers to the big house where the owner of the spread lives with his family (they're known as *haciendados*). Compared to the rough bunkhouses his men live in, the hacienda is an oasis of luxury, with whitewashed walls, tile roofs, a well of cool water for drinking, and maybe even a garden.

The Tombstone Epitaph's Guide to Mexico

The Mighty Rio Grande

The Rio Grande River makes up about half of the CSA-Mexico border. The Mexicans have never been happy about that; they prefer the former border, the Nueces River—tough luck for them. For a lot of its length, the Rio Grande is pretty shallow and slow moving; a man can wade or ride across it in a lot of places without too much trouble. The closer you get to the coast, the deeper and faster it gets; eventually the only ways across are swimming or by boat.

The region along the Rio Grande is pretty heavily settled. That water irrigates crops, keeps cattle healthy, and provides a living for a lot of folks. It's not always safe, though—a lot of folks drown in the Rio Grande every year and are washed away, or get eaten by jaguars or cougars that come to the river to drink.

84

Legion Border Garrisons

Since the Juaristas are so active in northern Mexico, the French Foreign Legion maintains several garrisons along the border and in the northern deserts. A company or two mans each garrison (a few are larger). Small villages, inhabited mainly by *taberneros* (*cantina*–saloon–keepers) and calico queens who cater to the Legionnaires, have sprung up around some of them.

As you're already aware, the Legionnaires tend to find these posts boring. Some of them have taken to relieving their boredom by marching out in small groups to harass and rob travelers on the Ghost Trail. I don't find that surprising, considering how many Legionnaires are convicts or murderers. It remains a big problem, since the Confederates can't catch them before they get back across the border to their home territory and their forts.

Northern Mexico

The border region blends imperceptibly into the northern part of Mexico, which mostly consists of the Sonora Desert. It looks just like the southwestern Confederacy—red rock, scrub brush, cacti, and canyons. Occasionally you run across a shallow river, or even a small, spring-fed lake. Some of those little grottoes are mighty pleasing to the eye.

A busy Mexican *hacienda*.

The Tombstone Epitaph's Guide to Mexico

Banditos Of The Sonora

Benito Juárez's men aren't the only ones who find the desert a good place to hide out. Plenty of banditos use the canyons and mesas for the same purpose. If you ride through that area, better make sure you bring some company—and that you're all good with shootin' irons.

Of all the bandits out there, the worst by far is a man who's known as *El Escorpión*—the Scorpion. I don't know what his real name is, and neither does anyone I talked to about it, not even the Rurales. However, I did get a description. He's supposed to be a devilishly handsome fellow with a broad smile and a well-groomed black moustache—not exactly your typical bandito, who's usually missing some teeth and carries more than a few scars.

Besides his looks, you can tell El Escorpión by his boastful manner. He can't resist talking about himself in the third person ("Now, El Escorpión will kill you!"), and he wears his personal scorpion emblem everywhere. It's engraved on the butts of his pistols, carved onto

The Tarhumara labor in a Spanish mine.

a big gold ring he wears, and even embroidered onto some of his clothes.

For all his good looks and fancy ways, El Escorpión's as cruel and lethal as his namesake's sting. He kills casually, almost as if he enjoys the sight of blood, and while he's got a reputation for refusing to harm ladies himself, he seems to have no qualms about turning them over to his men.

86

Vinegarroons

Speaking of scorpions, watch out for them while you travel through the desert, they're as thick there as ticks on a dog. Most of the time their sting's not fatal, but a few of them will drop you like a pole-axed steer. They love to crawl in empty boots and saddlebags and such and just wait for some poor fellow to stick a hand or foot in.

115

The deadliest of all the desert scorpions is a kind called a vinegarroon, because of the vinegar-like odor it gives off when you crush it. Vinegarroons can grow as big as your foot, and their sting can kill man or horse as quick as a gunshot between the eyes. It's not a pleasant death, either. I've seen men stung by these things scream like women because of the pain they felt as they died. If you see one of them, back off and shoot it, or crush it with a rock.

Copper Canyon

Earlier in my report I mentioned Copper Canyon, one of the northern desert's most prominent features. It's actually a series of gorges stretching from Los Mochis, on the northern coast of Sinaloa, almost to the city of Chihuahua. In places it's about a mile deep and a mile wide; a few places are deeper still, going further into the earth than even the Grand Canyon. The peaks rise as high as 8,000 feet. It's a beautiful, yet often desolate, country.

Spanish colonists discovered this place, and its inhabitants, the peaceful and semi-nomadic Tarahumara Indians, pretty early on. More to the point, they discovered that the canyon's caves contained silver. Before long there were plenty of mines in the Canyon, and Aztecs

The Tombstone Epitaph's Guide to Mexico

1877 Edition   "Believe it or Else!"   Only 10¢

and Tarahumara labored side by side in slavery to pull the silver out of the ground. I don't know how many thousands of them died there due to overwork, abuse, and disease.

Today there are still plenty of silver mines being worked in the region, though many have played out and been abandoned. Banditos sometimes use the latter as hideouts—and a few are no doubt the lairs of dangerous and frightening creatures.

Monterrey

The biggest and most important city of northern Mexico, and undoubtedly the best target for an initial strike by an invading Confederate army, is Monterrey, capital of the state of Nuevo León. Founded in 1596, it's known to the Mexicans as *El Sultán del Norte* ("Sultan of the North") because **88** of its industries and hellraising atmosphere.

Located amidst towering mountains, Monterrey makes a difficult military target. General Taylor found this out back in the Mexican-American War, when it took him four days to force the Mexican defenders to surrender.

The heart of the city, geographically at least, is a large cathedral built of a pale yellowish stone. The early Monterreyans began building it in 1600, but didn't finish it until about thirty years ago. On Sundays you can find just about everyone in town here, excepting the Legionnaires and the sorts of folks who cater to them. Located not far from the cathedral is the *Obispado,* a large residence where the Bishop of Monterrey used to live. These days it serves as the Legion's local headquarters.

Workin' For A Livin'

Monterrey has a booming economy based on many different industries. It's a center for silversmithing, since it's not far from the silver mines of Copper Canyon. Everything from silver jewelry, to fancy eating utensils, to silver-plated guns is available for sale in local shops. Glassmakers and crystal-makers also do a booming business, though a lot of what they produce is carefully packed up and shipped off by mule or wagon train to Mexico City, or even Texas. Several different brewers produce the famous Monterrey *cerveza.*

Tippin' Back A Few

If you want to try some of that local beer, stop in at one of the city's many cantinas. I don't think some of them ever close, in fact. If beer's not to your taste, try the local *sangria, tequila, mezcal,* or *pulque.* The latter three are types of fermented agave cactus juice which folks in Mexico have been drinking since Aztec times.

88

The first stage of fermentation gives you pulque, from that you can get mezcal, and then tequila's distilled from mezcal. If you can't pronounce these names, just ask for "cactus juice"; any Mexican barman will know what you mean. Watch out for these drinks, they'll rip the lining right out of your throat if you're not used to them—use a pinch of salt to cut the effect if you're lacking in fortitude. If you'd rather not risk the dangerous stuff, most cantinas and *pulquerias* have the usual assortment of rotgut whiskey, bourbon, and pretty *señoritas* that you can find in any other saloon north or south of the border.

For my taste, you can find the best beer and tequila at a place called Enrique's. Enrique Saldozar, the owner, brews the stuff himself. I don't know his secret, but his drinks are sweeter and harder than anywhere else in town. However, the Pepita de Plata and the La Linda (whose serving ladies live up to its name, "The Beauty") are both worth a stop too.

The Second Regiment

The Second Regiment, Third Battalion, First Brigade is based in Monterrey. Most Legionnaires consider this a plum assignment because of Monterrey's night life, and many try to get transferred into one of the Second Regiment's four companies.

The man in charge of all these "French" mercenaries is Major Kazimierz Zawicki, by birth a Pole. Unlike the usually lean and mean Legionnaire, he's a big, burly, slightly overweight fellow possessed of a sort of jovial bravado. He doesn't seem to like his offices in the Obispado much; you can usually find him at a table one of the local cantinas where the soldiers like to spend time, such as the Del Oro or the Hermosilla.

Santa Isabella

Located west of Monterrey, in the state of Coahuila not far from Saltillo and Parras, is a little place called Santa Isabella. Most Mexicans remember it fondly as the place where the Juaristas ambushed a company of Legionnaires in a defile back in 1872 and massacred every single one of them—nearly a hundred men—except for one Frenchie who lived to tell the tale.

I've been there, and I didn't like the "feel" of the place at all. I suspect the effects of the Reckoning have taken hold there in response to the slaughter—and whatever's risen up needs putting down pronto. I couldn't sense exactly what it was, so I think the problem needs a more thorough looking into.

Central Mexico

For my money, central Mexico's a damn sight nicer place than the northern part of the country. The climate cools down some, especially as you go up into the mountains, though it's still pretty warm most of the time. There's more water and a longer growing season. People are more plentiful, and generally friendlier.

Mexico City

The most important part of the central regions is, of course, the Valley of Mexico, which primarily means Mexico City. Of course, "Valley" is a sort of deceptive term—it is a valley in the middle of mountains, but it's over 7,000 feet in elevation, so the air can get a little thin for folks used to lower lands.

As I mentioned earlier in this report, Cortés built this place on the site of the Aztec capital, Tenochtitlan, after he filled in the lagoons. Using Aztec slave labor, he built the city in a European style, but along the old Aztec grid pattern. The Aztec ceremonial center became a public square ten acres in size paved with stones from the old Aztec main temple. It's called the *Zócalo* today. A lot of the buildings Cortés put up are made of *tezontle*, a volcanic rock with the disturbing color of dried blood—fitting tribute, I suppose, to all the Aztec sacrificial victims, and all the Indians Cortés butchered and enslaved.

Since Mexico City was built on top of a sort of swamp, the buildings don't always get the support they need. Some are noticeably "sunken" or just a few inches lopsided from years of sinking into the soft ground. Take a look at the Cathedral from across the Zócalo and you'll see what I mean.

The Zocalo

The center of Mexico City's civic life is the Zócalo (meaning "pedestal," so called from the bottom part of a statue Santa Anna began building but never finished back in 1843). It's big enough for everything from pleasant Sunday afternoon strolls, to political rallies, to military parades. Plenty of important buildings line its edges. The main building on the south side is the *Ayuntamiento*, or "city hall."

Cathedral Of Mexico

The grand Cathedral of Mexico dominates the northern side of the Zócalo. It took about three centuries to build, but it was worth it. It's got five altars and 14 chapels, mostly done in an elaborate, Spanish baroque style. Gold and jewels encrust much of the decor. Even if you're not religious, you can't help but be awed.

The National Palace

With the north devoted to the rule of God, the east of the Zócalo is more concerned with the rule of Man. The National Palace, a two-story building, is the seat of the Empire of Mexico—at least formally. The Empress doesn't like it much, though, so Maximillian and Carlotta spend most of their time at Chapultepec Castle. However, formal state occasions, including many of the elaborate balls the Empress likes to throw, take place here. Many government offices are located here as well. Because of all the unrest in the country, the Palace is guarded tighter than a drum most times, and even tighter when the Emperor is around.

The Tombstone Epitaph's Guide to Mexico

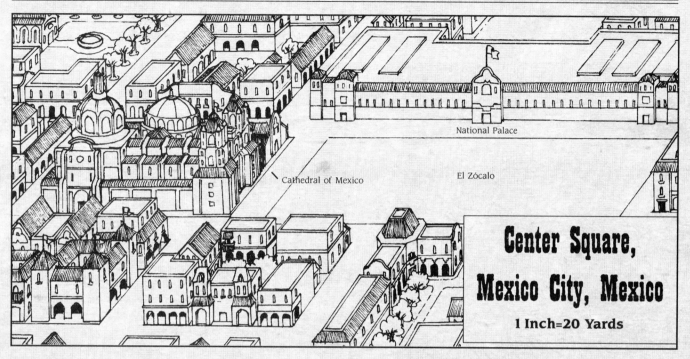

National Palace

Cathedral of Mexico   El Zócalo

Center Square, Mexico City, Mexico

1 Inch=20 Yards

The capitol, Mexico City.

Chapultepec Castle

Surrounded by 1,500-acre grounds said to be the most beautiful in all of Mexico, Chapultepec Castle is the imperial residence. It sits on *Cerro de Chapulín* ("Grasshopper Hill") so it can overlook most of the city.

An Aztec palace used to occupy this spot, then a gunpowder plant, then a military school where a famous battle of the Mexican-American War was fought. If you think the security at the National Palace is tight, just try getting into this place. The guards here are tough even for legionnaires.

The *Jardin Zoologica*

Emperor Montezuma used to have himself a zoo that not only was the envy of other chiefs, but astonished Cortés and his conquistadors. Where his used to be, now you'll find the state's Zoological Gardens—*Jardín Zoológica* in Spanish. It has creatures not only from Mexico, but Europe, Africa, and the Orient. It's said to be one of Empress Carlotta's favorite places to go. If you think you've seen everything strange there is to see, give this place a try—I bet it will prove you wrong.

Don't Wear Red

One of the main forms of entertainment in Mexico City, and in many other cities throughout the land, is *el corrida*—the bullfight. The bullfighting season typically runs from November to March, and the biggest and best fights are held on Saturday and Sunday afternoons. In Mexico City, these fights take place at the *Plaza Méjico*, where the country's largest *plaza de toros*, or bullring, is located.

I'm no *aficianado*—I don't think much of a sport where you shave down an animal's horns and stick its neck muscles full of spikes just so you can skewer it with a sword—but thousands of Mexicans are. Skilled *toreadors*, or bullfighters, have the same sort of popularity that singers and artists do over in Paris. More than a few have died in the bullring, but those who survive enough fights can retire wealthy and beloved.

Lately it seems that the bulls may be getting some revenge. A number of bodies have been found recently with large gore wounds. No one has seen the deaths occur, and no loose animals have been found that could have caused these wounds.

117

The Tombstone Epitaph's Guide to Mexico

1877 Edition   "Believe it or Else!"   Only 10¢

The Ruins Of Teotihuacan

91

One of the most interesting features of central Mexico is located in a valley just a short distance from Mexico City. It's the ruin of an enormous city called Teotihuacán which dates from pre-Aztec times—in fact, the Aztecs used it for rituals, and thought that their gods met there when they ignited the Fifth Sun. Covering as much as ten square miles, Teotihuacán was the center of a vast network of trade routes and had enormous cultural influence on the Zapotecs, Mayans, and other tribes.

The centerpiece of Teotihuacán is a long paved street, *Miccaotli*—the Avenue of the Dead—which connects a large pyramid, the Pyramid of the Moon, with an area known as the *Ciudadela* ("Citadel") which includes the Temple of Quetzalcoatl. About a third of the way down from the Pyramid of the Moon there's another pyramid, the Pyramid of the Sun. Both of the pyramids seem to have some astronomical significance; they align with the rising of the sun or certain stars on particular days.

Other buildings that have been excavated so far mainly appear to be house compounds (series of rooms in a roughly square shape around a central courtyard) or temples. Some beautiful murals depicting Mesoamerican gods have been uncovered. Many other important buildings no doubt exist underneath the nearby fields and hills, but Professor Riley tells me it will probably be decades before the area has been completely explored.

Guadalajara

Situated north and west of Mexico City, in the state of Jalisco, Guadalajara has always been a little isolated due to its location in the mile-high Antemajac Valley in the Sierra Madres. It has cliffs on three sides, and the 2,000-foot deep Oblatos Canyon on the other—making it not exactly the easiest place to reach.

Founded in 1532, Guadalajara became wealthy and powerful thanks to the farms and silver mines in the region. Because it was far away from the political centers of Mexico City and Veracruz, it developed an independent streak that you'll still find today in the *Tapatíos,* as the residents are known. Cross them or try to tell them what to do, and you'll learn pretty quick they don't tolerate being ordered around.

El Jefe

Fortunately, they at least had the sense to pick the toughest-minded, most stubborn cuss in town to be their *alcalde,* or mayor. Ramón Alphonso Delpaiz y Turino, better known simply as *El Toro*— "the Bull"—is enough of a man to stand up to even a Texas Ranger. He started off in life dirt poor, and eventually became a vaquero on one of the haciendas in the region. He saved his money, got into business, built up his popularity, and eventually got himself elected *alcalde.*

92

They say that Delpaiz used to wrestle steers to the ground with his bare hands, and I can just about believe it. He's not big—no taller than me, really—but he's as broad-shouldered as a barn, and as strong as a team of oxen. But that doesn't do him much good as mayor most of the time; for that job he's got to use his brains, and, fortunately for him, they seem just as strong.

Everyone in town knows that El Toro's in charge in Guadalajara. If you want to start a business, you get a permit from him (and probably end up paying him an annual kickback for permission to run it too). You break the wrong laws, and he'll personally trip the door on the scaffold when time comes for you to swing for it. Locals refer to the *Palacio Municipal* ("City Hall") as *El Castillo* ("The Castle") because of the heavy-handed way he runs things.

Houses O' The Lord

Guadalajara gets a lot of religious pilgrims every year, mainly to visit two important churches. The *Catedral,* consecrated in 1618, is the centerpiece of the town. It's got eleven magnificent altars—ten in silver and gold (the gifts of King Fernando VII of Spain), and the last in carved white marble from Italy (that one's only about 15 years old, in fact). The altar pieces, and the sacristy painting *The Assumption of the Virgin* by Murillo, possess both great beauty and great value. A special squad of guards, handpicked by the archbishop, protects the place.

The Tombstone Epitaph's Guide to Mexico

1877 Edition   "Believe it or Else!"   Only 10¢

More visitors go to the Basilica de la Virgen de Zapopan, though. It's the home of *La Zapoponita,* Our Lady of Zapopan. Our Lady is a ten-inch-tall statue of the Virgin Mary made of corn paste that supposedly causes miracles— spontaneous healings and so forth. I'm not so sure about that, but there did seem to be something unusual about it, so maybe it's all it's cracked up to be. From May to October, La Zapoponita tours the state, visiting every single parish church. When she returns to Guadalajara on October 12, there's an enormous street festival and celebration.

Lake O' Sorrow

Not too far from Guadalajara is a big lake, Lake Chapala. Situated in the middle of some towering mountains, it's always been a popular place for swimming, fishing, or just taking in the vista. Guadalajarans often row out to some of the lake's islands, such as Isla de los Alacranes (Scorpion Island) or Isla de Mezcala, to picnic.

Recently, though, several folks have disappeared in or around the lake—strong swimmers mysteriously drowned, or boats apparently capsized in fine weather. None of the bodies have ever washed ashore, though the lake's not known for strong undercurrents. If I had time, I'd investigate further, but for now, I must simply advise *Epitaph* readers not to go swimming there.

93

Veracruz

The other major city of central Mexico, and the other end of the axis of French-controlled Mexico, is Veracruz. Founded by Cortés, it's served as a gateway to Mexico for invaders ever since.

Veracruz has a very different feel from Mexico City. An influx of black slaves and Cubans early in its history has given it a more diverse culture. For example, a particular form of music, performed by trios of white-suited street guitarists, is unique to Veracruz.

93

However, the Frenchies are just as prevalent here as there. In order to keep a route to the sea open for French trade, the Legion has stationed several companies here, along with many regular French and Mex troops.

The sacred Zapoponista.

Veracruz is a hot, humid place. It gets drenched by rain just about every day during some parts of the year, so if you come, prepare for some storms. Even worse is the "norther," a fierce northern wind strong enough to blow ships aground and knock trees and houses down. It's no wonder the nearby ruins of Zempoala have a large circular temple to Ehécatl, the Aztec god of wind.

Walls And Forts

Veracruz used to be the chief Spanish port in Mexico—the one from which they shipped out all the gold and silver their Indian slaves were digging out of the ground. Naturally enough, this attracted pirates. More than once groups of well-armed pirates herded all of Veracruz's citizens onto nearby islands so that they could ransack the town in peace. Of course, the townsfolk got tired of this, and finally built some fortifications: the Fort of San Juan de Ulúa and the Baluarte Santiago.

What can be found at the bottom of this cenote?

The Fort is built on an island out in the bay itself; it's not connected to the mainland at all. Today it's used as a prison, and not a very pleasant one. I've heard that inmates die out there every day. Santa Anna once imprisoned Benito Juárez there, in fact. The place is supposed to be a maze of cellars, walls, ramparts, towers, moats, and drawbridges; *veracruzanos* say that even if someone managed to escape from his cell—which has never happened—he'd never be able to find his way off the island.

The Baluarte Santiago, on the other hand, is located on the mainland. It's a long wall, with a series of small forts, along the town's waterfront. It's a little bit rundown—it's hundreds of years old, after all—but Maximillian's people have been reinforcing it. The commander of the city's garrison, Colonel August Dupuis, seems to fear a seaborne invasion (from whom, I don't know, though I'm sure the Confederacy or the United States could certainly give it a try if necessary) and is determined to thwart it with the help of these fortifications.

93

Carnaval

But Veracruz isn't all rotten weather and old forts. Actually, the place can be pretty lively and exciting. Its biggest celebration is *Carnaval*, which takes place before Lent and is sort of Veracruz's version of Mardi Gras in New Orleans. Street parades, parties, costumes, music, and singing all take place during Carnaval.

My friend Elizardo Alarcón, who runs a cantina and a general store in town, tells me Carnaval isn't as exciting as it used to be. The past few years, someone's been spoiling the mood. Fights have broken out more frequently, and every year a few slit-throated bodies or two are found in alleys when it's all over.

Los Hermanos

Personally, I think you can trace the Carnaval problems to a large gang of robbers, thugs, and bully-boys called Los Hermanos ("The Brothers"). These ne'er-do-wells have been making trouble in Veracruz ever since I've been going down there. They're walking a little more softly these days, with the Legion around and all, but when the Frenchies aren't looking, they still rustle cattle, steal from shopkeepers, rough up anyone they don't like, and raise ever-loving Hell.

An ugly little fellow named Efraín Alejo-Esparza runs Los Hermanos. He's not the sort of guy you'd pick to lead a gang of legbreakers and cut-throats; most of his fellow Hermanos stand at least two or three inches taller than he. But he's meaner and crueller than any five of them put together. He's the Devil himself with a knife. Anyone who gets into a knife-fight with him ends up carved to ribbons, and he can throw one fast and accurately enough to put it between some gunslinger's eyes before the other fellow can even clear leather. The meanest members of Los Hermanos speak softly and respectfully to him.

Los Hermanos usually polish their pistols down at a little cantina called Felina's, near the waterfront. If you go in there, you'd better be prepared to kowtow to them; they don't take any lip in their own place. Even if you meet them in other bars around town—and you will—they're not likely to put up with anything their *macho* natures regard as an insult.

The Tombstone Epitaph's Guide to Mexico

1877 Edition   "Believe it or Else!"   Only 10¢

Casa de Lebron

The last place I'll mention in central Mexico, since it may have some strategic significance, is located between Mexico City and Veracruz, in the state of Puebla—not far, in fact, from the town of Puebla, where the Mexicans initially fought off the French. It's *Casa de Lebron*—Santa Anna's ancestral *hacienda*.

Santa Anna's family's been living at this place, one of the largest and wealthiest ranches in Mexico, literally for centuries. It's got dozens of servants, hundreds of acres of land, and more cattle and horses than you can count. These days, it's got guards, too—Mex soldiers, none of those French boys. I've heard that the fields are worked at night by some "veterans" of Santa Anna's Army of the Dead, but I haven't seen any.

Santa Anna supposedly returns to his *hacienda* whenever he gets a little break from the action up in California. Now that it seems he's preparing to invade the state by force, I doubt you'll see him back down here anytime soon.

Southern Mexico

Like the coastal area around Veracruz, southern Mexico tends to be warm and humid. Unless you get a little elevation underneath your feet up in the mountains, where it can be pretty pleasant sometimes, you're likely to be hot and miserable a lot of the time.

Much of this part of the country, particularly the Yucatán Peninsula, is covered in jungle. One of the reasons Professor Riley and his compatriots know so little about the Mayan people is that their cities and such are hidden beneath acres of jungle trees and vines.

Cenotes

Some of the relics of the Maya civilization we do know about are special "sacrificial wells" called *cenotes*. The Yucatán Peninsula region has a lot of limestone which is riddled with underground caverns. When one of these caverns collapses, it forms a natural "well" which soon collects water. Although they did use them for drinking and bathing water, the Mayans considered cenotes sacred (as did the Toltecs, who once invaded and controlled this area), and used them for sacrifices.

95

For minor matters, precious objects would be thrown into the wells. For major matters, it would be people, often young women. Professor Riley tells me that some of the things they've dredged from cenotes include little rubber dolls, human and animal bones, disks and jewelry made of gold or jade, statuettes, pottery, and many other objects.

A few cenotes were thought to be gates into Xibalbá, the Mayan underworld. Those were avoided at all costs. Even today, peasants give them a wide berth.

Good Hunting

The jungles and rain forests of southern Mexico have always been good hunting grounds; the Maya term for part of the region is "The Land of Turkey and Deer." Today, besides food animals, you can also hunt the strange creatures of the Reckoning. And that's brought the Explorer's Society to this neck of the woods.

Led by a local Explorer, Don Felipe Alvarez-Pereira de Roque y Oseguera, the scion of an old Spanish family, members of the Society have been "jaunting" down here, as they say, to go hunting for everything from jaguars to naguals, feathered serpents, and Mictlan owls. Personally, it doesn't strike me as the best hobby, but to each his own, I suppose.

Don Felipe's magnificent hacienda, located on a cliff top overlooking a waterfall and a verdant jungle, serves as the Explorer's Society local headquarters. At any given time at least a couple of them are likely to be occupying Don Felipe's guest quarters. The heads and horns arranged along the Don's walls are mute testimony to their hunting skills.

Despite his hazardous pastime, Don Felipe is a gracious host and always has time to entertain weary travelers. If you happen to be traveling in this area stop by his hacienda for a visit. In exchange for stories of your travels Don Felipe will provide a comfortable place to spend the night and some of the finest cuisine to be found south of the border.

CHAPTER TWO:
MAKIN' MEXICANS

Okay, pardner, here's where you get the God's-honest on creating Mexican characters. For the most part, it's not all that different from creating characters from any other place, so don't expect this chapter to be real long or anything, but there are a few useful bits of information you need to know.

CLASS AND RACE

Although it's not nearly as bad as it was a hundred or two hundred years ago, Mexico is still a class-based society in many ways. The "haves" run things, and the "have nots" do as they're told. Benito Juárez tried to put a stop to the worst parts of this system, and as a result the rich and powerful turned against him.

PENINSULARES

At the top of the pecking order are the *peninsulares* ("people of the peninsula"), also called *gachupines* ("spur-wearers"). These used to be folks who were born in Spain (the Iberian Peninsula, hence the name) and then came over to Mexico. Today, it can still mean that, but it's more likely to mean someone directly descended from that sort of person—a "Mexican" whose forebears were all born in Spain, or born to parents whose ancestors never married any native Mexicans. This has led to a lot of intermingling between various "noble" families, but so far this doesn't seem to have had any really bad effects across the board. There may be a few dim-witted, hairy-palmed "cousins" hidden away in hacienda basements, but if so, no one talks about them.

In the colonial period, the peninsulares controlled everything—the government, the church, the army, the land, you name it. Today, they don't have quite that level of dominance, but they do own most of the land, control most of the wealth, and hold most of the top positions in the government and the army (aside from the French, of course). They're

Peninsulares and, to a lesser extent, criollos are often referred to by specific titles and terms. Men are called "Don" (Sir), and women Doña (Lady), as in Don Felipe, who's mentioned near the end of the *Epitaph* report. Women could also be called *dama* (lady), and men *caballero* (gentleman or horseman).

MESTIZOS

Separated from peninsulare and criollo by a considerable social gulf are *mestizos*, persons of mixed Spanish and Indian blood. This includes most Mexicans, who have at least a *little* Indian blood in them. Sometimes this term also applies to Indians who abandon their native ways and adopt those of the white man. Unlike full-blooded Indians, or blacks, mestizos are considered reasoned and civilized people, and can often advance quite far in society.

Mestizos have one thing which their "betters" don't, though—their own type of arcane powers. See *City Of Lost Angels*, for information on mestizo Anahuac magic.

CAMPESINOS, INDIANS, AND BLACKS

At the very bottom of the social ladder are *campesinos* (farmers, countrymen, and peasants), Indians, and blacks—all of whom have relatively little power in society. This class includes *mulattos* (offsprings of a Spaniard and a black) and *zambos* (offspring of a black and an Indian). Of particular note are *cimarrones*, or "maroons," free blacks descended from escaped slaves. They live in isolated communities, typically in the south, and have little regard for strangers.

SOCIAL CLASS

In game terms, a character's class within Mexican society is represented with an Edge (or Hindrance in the case of Indians and blacks). Keep in mind that a Mexican character's social standing usually means beans outside of Mexico (though it may have some pull in Central or South America, where similar systems often exist).

particularly prevalent in the Church; pretty much every bishop or higher-ranking Church official was born in Spain, or has parents who were.

CRIOLLOS

One step down the social ladder are the *criollos*. Originally, this term meant persons of Spanish ancestry born in the New World. Today, it's been broadened to mean any affluent or successful Mexican. Doctors, lawyers, most bureaucrats, teachers, many priests, and the owners of factories and other economic assets usually fall into this social class. They ape the peninsulares by wearing similar clothing and trying to follow upper-class fashions. Despite this, the peninsulares consider the criollos of inferior stock.

HINDRANCES AND EDGES

Here are some notes on existing Hindrances and Edges, along with a couple of new ones for heroes south of the border.

HINDRANCES

Here are some new ways to scrape out some extra points and Fate chips for your hero. Use them wisely, or we'll find you.

MACHO   3

A key element of Latin culture is the concept of *machismo*: men will be manly and women exist to serve and pleasure them. Your hero cannot let any slight to his honor or manhood go unchallenged, and women are merely pretty objects there for your enjoyment. Your hombre views himself as the epitome of manliness and virility. This can occasionally ruffle some feathers in Mexico, but north of the border it may get your hero shot by someone who doesn't share his views.

This Hindrance is only available to male heroes.

OLD HINDRANCES

Big 'Un, Brawny: These Hindrances tend to be uncommon among Mexicans, who are, on the average, shorter than folks north of the border.

Ferner: This one ain't appropriate for Mexicans in their homeland, of course, but it's perfect for all those French visitors and soldiers. Indians who've held to their native ways, yet now find themselves living mainly among regular Mexicans, might take the *ferner* Hindrance as well.

Greedy: Many peninsulares and criollos have this Hindrance.

Intolerance: Most Mexicans can get along all right with members of classes lower than theirs, even if they may not like it all the time. But some are downright cruel towards anyone who doesn't meet their "standards," and *intolerance* (at the 3-point level) reflects this.

Poverty: Most characters with the *social class* Hindrance also have this Hindrance. Many mestizos also take this Hindrance.

Tinhorn: Many peninsulares have this Hindrance. They've lived such sheltered lives, and take such pride in their ancestry, that they can't handle themselves away from haciendas and cities. This Hindrance is also appropriate for European visitors, like ambassadors, military observers, and traders, who have taken up temporary residence in Mexico.

EDGES

Here are a few ways to give your hombre a leg up on the competition. As nasty as things can get down south, you'll need them.

FUERO   3

Fuero is a new Edge for characters in the military or the Church. It represents their right to be tried for crimes only in military or ecclesiastical court, respectively—and, naturally enough, such courts are often more likely to rule in their favor than for some poor peon. Benito Juárez abolished this legal privilege; Emperor Maximillian, though not well-regarded by the Church because of his failure to restore its lands, at least restored the *fueros*.

SOCIAL CLASS

Value	Edge
1	Mestizo
2	Criollo
3	Peninsulare

Value	Hindrance
-2	Campesino, Indian, black, mulatto, zambo, or cimarrone

CHASSEPOT RIFLE

Weapon	Ammo	Shots	ROF	Range	Damage	QD	Con	Cost
Chassepot	11mm	1	1	25	5d8	-1	6	$20

OLD EDGES

Belongings, Dinero, Friends In High Places: Virtually all peninsulares, and many criollos, have one or all of these Edges. Superb horses and weapons are among the most common *belongings*. Most peninsulares usually have contacts in the government upon which they can call. Some may also have contacts among the rebels.

Law Man, Rank: Rurales have *law man* at level 4, and *rank* at level 0.

NAMIN' YOUR HOMBRE

We're not talking about any old Tom, Dick, and Harry here, you know. It's more like any Tomás, Ricardo, or Geraldo.

And Mexicans set great store by names—they can tell you a lot about a person and his family—so you'd better get 'em right. Family honor is still a highly cherished value, especially among the peninsulares.

FAMILY NAMES

Spanish names are written with the person's given name first, and his family name second, just like English names. An hombres' last names are derived from the surnames of both of a person's parents, with the father's name coming first.

If Ricardo Arenas-Esparza and Estrella Fernando-Torres marry, her name changes to Estrella Fernando de Arenas (she drops her mother's maiden name, Torres, and adds her husband's first surname; some women would write it "Fernando-Arenas"). Their children will have the surname Arenas-Fernando (or Arenas y Fernando).

Here's a brief—very brief—selection of Spanish surnames and given names you can use. That way all of your Mexican characters don't end up named Juan and Maria.

SPANISH NAMES

It's time to go to town and name your hombre.

FAMILY NAMES

Choose your heroes last names from among these fine choices. Don't forget that you'll need two.

Acevedo
Acosta
Agaza
Aguilar
Alamar
Alarcón
Alejandro
Alemán
Almeida
Alonso
Alvarado
Alvarez
Anaya
Aquino
Aragon
Aragones
Arancon
Arellano
Arenas
Avila
Ayala
Ayarza
Azevedo
Balzano
Barajas
Barraza
Bascaro
Bastos
Batista
Benitez
Bermudez
Buenaflor
Cabrales
Cabranes
Cabrera
Calderón
Camarena
Campino
Campos
Carasquillo
Cardoza
Casillas

Castillo
Cifuentes
Contreras
Cordova
Costilla
Cuevas
Chavez
Davalos
Diaz
Dominguez
Duran
Echevarria
Elizondo
Escalante
Escobedo
Espinoza
Esposito
Esquivel
Fernandez
Feliciano
Flores
Fonseca
Fuentes
Gallegos
Gimenez
Gomez
Gonzalez
Grijalva
Gutierrez
Guzmán
Hernandez
Herrera
Izquierdo
Juarez
Landrón
Linares
Lopez
Lorenzo
Lozano
Lucero
Malindez
Mariano
Marquez
Martinez
Melendez
Mendoza
Menendez
Montalvo
Morales
Murietta
Narvaez

Olagues
Olivencia
Orlando
Orozco
Ortega
Ortiz
Paz
Pedrosa
Pena
Perales
Pereira
Pérez
Quiñones
Quintana
Quintero
Ramirez
Reyes
Reynoso
Rivera
Robles
Rodriguez
Rojas
Romero
Rosales
Sabado
Salvador
Sanchez
Sandoval
Santana
Santiago
Sepúlveda
Silverio
Soriano
Suarez
Tejada
Torres
Trujillo
Urabazo
Urquidez
Valdez
Valente
Valenzuela
Vega
Velasco
Villanueva
Villareál
Villegas
Zambrano
Zamora
Zapata
Zavala

Male Given Names

Pick a first name for your Don.

Abelardo
Abraham
Alberto
Alejandro
Alfonso
Alfredo
Alonzo
Alphonso
Alvarado
Andrés
Angel
Antonio
Armando
Augustín
Bernardo
Calixto
Carlos
Celestino
César
Claudio
Cristobal
Delfino
Diego
Domingo
Eduardo
Edwin
Efraín
Emílio
Enrique
Esteban
Felipe
Fernando
Gabriél
Gaspar
Geraldo
Gilberto
Guillermo
Gustavo
Hector
Hernando
Horacio
Illuminado
Ismael
Itamar
Jaime
Javier
Jesús

Joaquin
Jorge
José
Juan
Lauro
Lazaro
Leon
Manuel
Marco
Mario
Martín
Mauricio
Miguel
Nestor
Orlando
Osvaldo
Pancho
Pascual
Ramón
Raphael
Raúl
Reymundo
Reynaldo
Ricardo
Rico
Roberto
Rodolfo
Rodrigo
Salvadór
Samuel
Santiago
Santos
Silverio
Timoteo
Tomás

Female Given Names

Pick a first name for your Dama.

Ada
Adela
Alicia
Alma
Amada
Andrea
Anita
Anna
Aracel

Bárbara
Blanca
Carmen
Catalina
Cecilia
Christina
Clara
Concepción
Conchita
Constanza
Consuela
Delores
Dona
Efigenia
Emma
Estella
Esperanza
Eugenia
Evangelina
Evita
Felicita
Felina
Gabriella
Inez
Isabel
Juanita
Leonora
Linda
Lina
Lola
Lucia
Lucila
Luisa
Lupe
Luz
Lydia
Margarita
Maria
Marisol
Mercedes
Paula
Petra
Ramona
Rita
Rosa
Rosalinda
Rosaria
Rosita
Roxana
Susana
Sylvia
Teresa
Violeta
Yolanda

MEXICAN REBEL

TRAITS & APTITUDES

Deftness 2d12
   Shootin': pistol, rifle 4
Nimbleness 2d10
   Climbin' 1
   Dodge 2
   Fightin': brawlin' 2
   Horse-ridin' 2
   Sneak 2
Quickness 3d10
Strength 3d6
Vigor 4d8
Cognition 3d8
   Scrutinize 2
   Search 2
   Trackin' 2
Knowledge 3d6
   Area knowledge: home
      state 2
   Spanish 2d6
Mien 4d6
   Overawe 2
Smarts 2d6
   Scroungin' 1
   Survival (desert) 2
Spirit 2d6
   Guts 2
Wind: 14
Edges:
   Social class: mestizo 1
Hindrances:
   Outlaw –3
   Yearnin' (to free Mexico) –5
Gear: Navy Pistol, Henry
   Repeating Rifle, 20 rounds
   of ammunition for both
   guns, knife, rope, horse,
   saddle, blanket, 53 pesos.

PERSONALITY

I fight, but I fight for freedom and justice for *all* Mexicans—not just the wealthy, or the military, but all of us. For too long all power and wealth has been in the hands of just a few men who controlled all of our lives, and now those men are not even Mexicans. It is time to fight back and take what is rightfully ours, and drive the foreign invaders from our soil!

Life in the desert is a hard one, between soldiers chasing you, bandits trying to hunt you down for a bounty, and some of the creatures that live here. But it's the only choice open to us right now. If *Jefe* Juárez can tolerate it at his age, so can I.

Quote: *"¡Viva Juárez! Vive liberdad! Viva Méjico!"*

Deserter

Traits & Aptitudes

Deftness 3d10
  Shootin': rifle 3
Nimbleness 2d12
  Climbin' 1
  Dodge 2
  Fightin': brawlin, saber 4
  Sneak 1
Strength 3d10
Quickness 3d6
Vigor 4d6
Cognition 2d6
  Artillery (cannons) 1
  Scrutinize 1
  Search 1
Knowledge 2d6
  Academia (military theory) 1
  Area knowledge: home area 2
  Native language 2
  French 1
  Spanish 1
  Professional (player's
    choice) 2
Mien 2d8
  Overawe 2
Smarts 2d8
  Gamblin' 1
  Survival (desert) 3
Spirit 2d6
Wind: 14
Edges:
  Sand 3
  Tough as nails 1
Hindrances:
  Bloodthirsty –2
  Ferner –3
  Enemy: the Legion –3
Gear: Chassepot, Smith & Wesson No.
  3 revolver, 30 rounds of ammunition
  for both guns, canteen, two weeks'
  worth of food, 25 pesos.

Personality

Oui, I was of the Legion, but I got tired of the way they treated me. Don't they understand what's going on in this world? It is no longer the way it used to be. Now monsters walk in broad daylight, and still they have us fight for puppet rulers and the glory of France!

Certainment, I know the penalties for desertion from the French Foreign Legion. Don't you worry about me, *m'sieur.* I can take care of myself. The Legion taught me how.

Quote: "Surrender? *Merde!* I never surrender!"

No Man's
Land

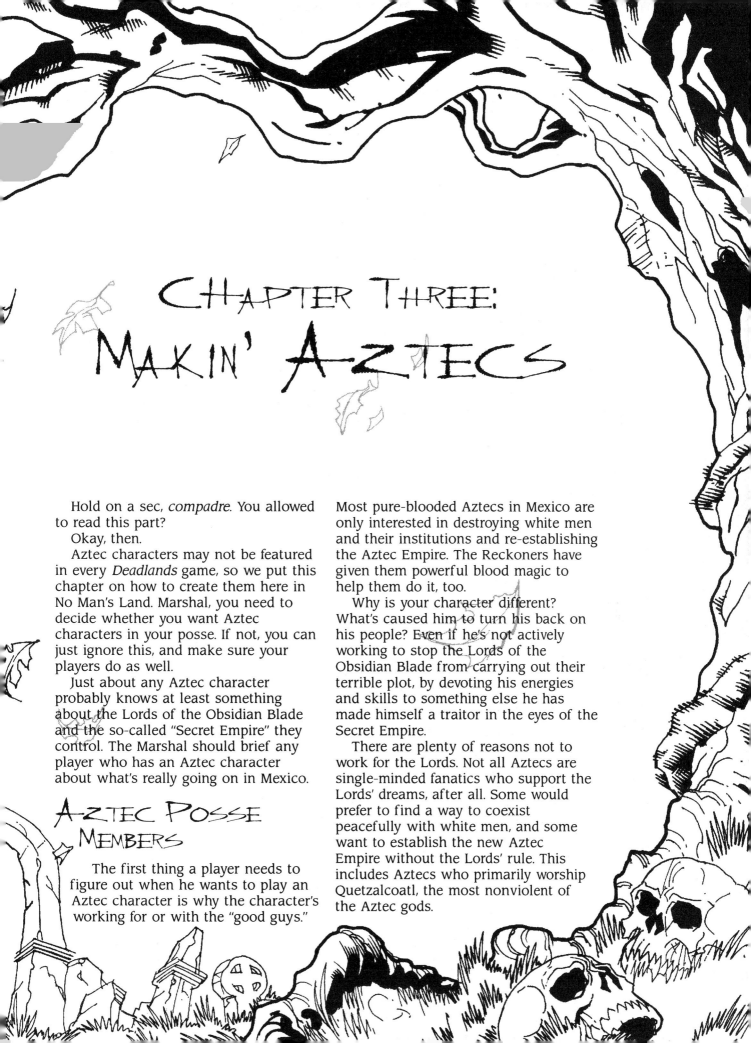

CHAPTER THREE:
MAKIN' AZTECS

Hold on a sec, *compadre*. You allowed to read this part?

Okay, then.

Aztec characters may not be featured in every *Deadlands* game, so we put this chapter on how to create them here in No Man's Land. Marshal, you need to decide whether you want Aztec characters in your posse. If not, you can just ignore this, and make sure your players do as well.

Just about any Aztec character probably knows at least something about the Lords of the Obsidian Blade and the so-called "Secret Empire" they control. The Marshal should brief any player who has an Aztec character about what's really going on in Mexico.

AZTEC POSSE MEMBERS

The first thing a player needs to figure out when he wants to play an Aztec character is why the character's working for or with the "good guys."

Most pure-blooded Aztecs in Mexico are only interested in destroying white men and their institutions and re-establishing the Aztec Empire. The Reckoners have given them powerful blood magic to help them do it, too.

Why is your character different? What's caused him to turn his back on his people? Even if he's not actively working to stop the Lords of the Obsidian Blade from carrying out their terrible plot, by devoting his energies and skills to something else he has made himself a traitor in the eyes of the Secret Empire.

There are plenty of reasons not to work for the Lords. Not all Aztecs are single-minded fanatics who support the Lords' dreams, after all. Some would prefer to find a way to coexist peacefully with white men, and some want to establish the new Aztec Empire without the Lords' rule. This includes Aztecs who primarily worship Quetzalcoatl, the most nonviolent of the Aztec gods.

exterminate it, for example. Thus, Aztec posse members will typically make some effort to hide the fact of the Secret Empire's existence, even if they do not support it.

They may claim to be resurrecting their peoples' ancient beliefs in the spirit of the Old Ways movement, or to be part of a small group of survivors who hid in an isolated mountain valley. But they will rarely, if ever, reveal the existence of the Secret Empire to non-Aztecs until it's absolutely necessary to do so.

CREATING AZTEC CHARACTERS

When building an Aztec character, you need a slightly different mindset than when building most Weird West characters. Aztecs are Indians, but very unlike the Indians described in *Deadlands* and *Ghost Dancers* for the most part. Their civilization is much older and more complex. They built cities that astounded Europeans. Their mythology, lore, and science were all very advanced in many ways, even by white standards. And that was 350 years ago; though they've lived in secret since then, they've preserved, and even advanced, most of their practices and learning.

So, don't think of it quite like building an Indian character (such as a brave or shaman) and then "civilizing" him. It's more appropriate to think of building a character from a very different, but no less civilized, society that happens to bear some faint resemblance to Indian societies.

Most Aztec posse members will fall into one of two types: warriors (often "elite" ones, such as Jaguar Knights or otontin); and priests of benign gods such as Quetzalcoatl. Many professions which once played an important part in Aztec society (such as traveling merchants) really don't have a place anymore, or wouldn't be appropriate as posse members. Servants of Tezcatlipoca and other dark gods are also not appropriate as heroes.

Others may have been betrayed by the Lords, or may have recently discovered the truth of where their power comes from and decided such evil cannot be tolerated (Aztec religion may look savage and evil to white men, but at it's heart it's nothing of the sort—it's just very, very different from European religions).

AZTECS AND NORMAL SOCIETY

If it became widely known that a substantial number of pure-blooded Aztecs still exist, and still maintain their traditional culture, it could have a devastating effect on that culture. The Mexican authorities would, rightly, perceive it as a threat and try to

New Hindrances

Some new Hindrances and Edges are needed to represent Aztec characters faithfully, and some existing ones have special implications or uses for Aztecs.

Bad Birth Omens 3/5

Some Aztecs have the misfortune to be born on days which are unlucky in the Aztec calendar. For -3 points, the character goes bust when half of his dice come up 1s. For -5 points, the character also suffers the effects of *bad luck*.

Blood Sacrifice 2

Some Aztec characters, including all priests, make daily sacrifices of blood as a way of propitiating the gods. This typically involves drawing a maguey thorn, obsidian needle, or similar sharp object through one's earlobe, tongue, genitals, or other body parts. Characters with this Hindrance must make such sacrifices, which cause them to suffer 1d4 points of Wind (don't reroll aces) which cannot be recovered for 24 hours. If a character fails to make his daily sacrifice, all rolls he makes suffer a -1 penalty due to the gods' displeasure.

Opoche 2

Opoche means "left-handed." In Aztec thought, it signifies someone other people consider sinister and untrustworthy. An Aztec character with this Hindrance suffers a -4 penalty to all *persuasion* rolls (or similar social interaction rolls) made against other Aztecs, unless those persuasion rolls are somehow based on threats or intimidation.

Old Hindrances

All Thumbs: Few Aztecs like, or are comfortable with, machines and scientific devices. Many of them take this Hindrance.

Enemy: All Aztecs who reject the goals of the Secret Empire earn its enmity. If the character actually works against the Lords of the Obsidian Blade, it's a -5 Hindrance. If he simply doesn't

want to have anything to do with them, it's -3. If the character spends substantial amounts of time outside of Mexico, reduce the value of the Hindrance accordingly.

Ferner: An Aztec who spends most of his time in white man's society may need to take this Hindrance.

Habit: Many Aztec priests do not bathe regularly, especially during certain sacred times. This can be considered a -1 Habit.

Old Ways Vow: This Hindrance is not required for any Aztec, though many do take it.

Superstitious: Most Aztecs take this Hindrance, since their lives are ruled by the lore and omens of the priests. The player should read up on Aztec myth and folklore so he can roleplay the character properly.

New Edge

Here's a new way to cheat the Marshal out of some fun.

Good Birth Omens 5

The opposite of *bad birth omens*, this Edge signifies a character who was born on one of the Aztec calendar's lucky days. The character only goes bust when 75% or more (round down) of his dice come up 1s. In addition the hero also gets to draw a chip whenever he gets 5 or more raises on an Aptitude roll.

Old Edges

Arcane Background: Aztec priests must take *arcane background: Aztec* to use their powers.

Aptitudes

A few Aptitudes have special significance for Aztecs.

Arts: Special Aztec arts include featherworking, goldsmithing, jadeworking, and obsidianworking.

Bow: Aztecs generally don't use bows; if they need to fight at a distance, they use *throwin': spear* (see below).

Fightin': Aztec warriors learn *fightin': macahuitl* to use their special weapons . A macahuitl cannot be quick-drawn; it's so cumbersome it has to be carried in the hands all the time anyway.

Horse Ridin': The Aztecs had never seen a horse until the Spaniards brought them to the New World. To this day they don't like them, and rarely learn to ride.

Language: The native Aztec tongue is Nahuatl. They've got to spend points to learn Spanish or English. Of course, almost no one else can understand them when they talk to each other.

Throwin': Aztecs often use a device called an *atlatl* which extends the range of a thrown spear. Spears thrown in this way have a Range Increment of 10. However, using one requires the character to know *throwin': atlatl* in addition to whatever Concentration he needs to throw the weapon without the atlatl.

Trade: Aztecs use *trade: obsidian flaking* to create the obsidian blades used in macahuitls, spears, and various sacrificial rituals.

Aztec Priests

Although the magical powers of Aztec priests aren't exactly the same as those of a Sioux, Apache, or Kiowa shaman, they're close enough in game terms to be represented with more or less the same rules. Aztec priests must buy *arcane background: Aztec,* not *shaman,* though.

The Aztec Gods

Aztec priests don't have animal totems or guardian spirits like most Indians. Instead, they worship gods (see Chapter One for descriptions). Aztec priests must choose a patron deity whom they particularly follow. They must make certain obeisances to all of the gods, but they follow the philosophies of one more than others.

For posse member Aztec priests, this patron god will almost always be one of the following, none of whom require human sacrifice in the *Deadlands* setting: Quetzalcoatl (god of learning, culture, wisdom, and the wind), Huehuecoyotl ("Old Coyote," a trickster god), Ometecuhtli (Lord of Duality, a creator god), Patecatl (god of medicine and healing), Xochipilli (god of pleasure, games, and frivolity), or Xochiquetzal (goddess of flowers and craftsmen). The other gods are not appropriate for heroes.

The priest must wear the regalia appropriate to his patron deity at most times. For example, a Quetzalcoatl priest would wear a feathered cloak, while an Ometecuhtli priest would wear clothing which simulated the attributes of that god. Thus, it will be easy for other Aztecs, or anyone with *academia: Aztec culture and lore,* to recognize which god an Aztec priest follows.

SACRED DAYS

In the Aztec calendar, certain days (and sometimes even certain hours) are sacred to certain gods. This makes it easier to obtain favors from them on those days. For each day in the game, ask your Marshal to roll 1d20. If he rolls a 1, that day is sacred to your character's patron god, and all favors requested from him have a -1 Appeasement cost (minimum of 1 Appeasement). After a sacred day, you must wait at least 20 days before asking the Marshal to check for other sacred days.

RITUALS

The following rituals generally are not used by Aztec priests: *animal spirit sacrifice, sand painting, spirit song, sweat lodge, tattoo.*

The following rituals are used in special, or slightly different, ways. If not listed here or above, a ritual may be used as described in *Ghost Dancers.*

Fast: While fasting, Aztec priests must also go without bathing. This gives them a -2 to *persuasion* rolls made against non-Aztecs (if the priest has the *habit* Hindrance, use its modifier instead).

Maim: As you might expect from the *blood sacrifice* Hindrance described above, not to mention the other descriptions of Aztec philosophy and religious practices found elsewhere in this book, the *maim* ritual is favored by Aztec priests and their gods.

Aztec priests cut or perforate themselves, allow the blood to drip onto sacred paper, and then burn the paper so that the essence of the blood wafts up to the gods amid the smoke. They do not, however, actually lop off any body parts—the Aztec gods need blood to survive, not eyes, ears, and fingers. The

amount of Appeasement received depends upon how much blood is sacrificed (described in terms of Wounds).

Favors, hexes, or other mystical means cannot cure Wounds suffered from Maiming. They must be allowed to heal naturally or the gods do not consider them a proper sacrifice. (simple medical care, such as herbal poultices, may still be applied).

Paint: Aztec priests use *paint* to create murals inside temple buildings (if available), or to create elaborate codices—mythological and/or historical books painted on crude paper bound together accordion-style.

Pledge: Aztec priests *pledge* to respect and honor specific Aztec deities (not nature spirits), and to offer blood and other sacrifices to them.

FAVORS

Generally, Aztec priests can use any of the favors listed in *Ghost Dancers,* though they should be re-conceptualized to fit Aztec mythology, lore, superstition, and philosophy. For example, *horned owl's fury* might become *eagle's fury,* since owls are typically regarded as evil omens, whereas eagles are sacred. *Lightning strike* would become *Tlaloc's dart* (it's perceived as an attack by the god of rain); and *earth speak* would be *favor of Tlaltecuhtli.*

Aztec priests rarely use the *visionseeking medicine way.* The *ghost medicine way* is also uncommon. Its magics are more associated with evil Aztec sorcerers.

 AZTEC MAIMING

Blood	Speed	TN	Appeasement
Light Wound	1	11	3
Heavy Wound	2	7	5
Serious Wound	4	5	7

AZTEC NAMES

Roll	Number	Day Sign
1	1 (Ce)	Reed (Acatl)
2	2 (Ome)	Jaguar (Ocelotl)
3	3 (Ye)	Eagle (Cuautli)
4	4 (Naui)	Vulture (Cozcacuahtli)
5	5 (Macuilli)	Motion (Earthquake) (Ollin)
6	6 (Chicace)	Flint (Tecpatl)
7	7 (Chicome)	Rain (Quiahuitl)
8	8 (Chicuei)	Flower (Xochitl)
9	9 (Chiconaui)	Crocodile (Cipactli)
10	10 (Matlactli)	Wind (Ehécatl)
11	11 (Matlactli Oce)	House (Calli)
12	12 (Matlactli Omome)	Lizard (Cuetzpallin)
13	13 (Matlactli Omei)	Snake (Coatl)
14		Death (Miquiztli)
15		Deer (Mazatl)
16		Rabbit (Tochtli)
17		Water (Atl)
18		Dog (Itzcuintli)
19		Monkey (Ozomatli)
20		Grass (Malinalli)

AZTEC WEAPONS

Weapon	DB	Damage	Range	Price
Macahuitl, 1-Handed				
Club	–	STR+1d4	–	$5
Obsidian Blade	–	STR+2d8	–	$15
Macahuitl, 2-Handed				
Club	+1	STR+1d8	–	$10
Obsidian Blade	–	STR+3d8	–	$30
Obsidian-Tipped Spear	+3	STR+2d6	10	$5
Dart	–	STR+1d4	5	$3
Atlatl	–	–	10	$5

AZTEC ARMOR

Armor	Armor Protection	Price
Ichcauipilli	-3 light armor	$20
Tlauiztli	-6 light armor	$50
Shield	+2 Defensive Bonus	$15

NAMING YOUR AZTEC

Aztec characters are typically named after the day they're born on in the Aztec sacred calendar (though someone born on an unlucky day may have his naming "delayed" until a lucky day in the hopes of tricking the gods into granting him good fortune).

This means that names consist of a number from 1 to 13, and one of twenty day-signs. You can use the following tables to pick a name for your hero randomly by rolling 1d20 twice, or simply choose a combination you like. (For the number, roll 1d20, but reroll numbers over 13.)

Hal is creating an Aztec warrior character and decides to determine his name randomly (after all, what control did the character have over which day he was born on?). He rolls 1d20 for the day's number. He gets a 16, so he rerolls, getting an 8. Then he rolls for a day-sign and gets 15, Deer. Thus, his character's name is Eight Deer (or Chicuei Mazatl, in Nahuatl).

AZTEC GEAR

The stats for Aztec weapons and armor are listed in the adjacent tables. The prices listed for them are for the cost when buying them as part of a hero's starting equipment. Once your character has begun her career as an adventurer, these items are much harder to come by. They must be made by an Aztec (your hero qualifies if she has the appropriate Aptitudes), or purchased from another Aztec via negotiation and barter.

Heroes using this gear must remember that the Aztec civilization is believed long dead by most Mexicans. Wandering around in full Aztec regalia may raise some eyebrows and lead to some unpleasant questions (and some unpleasant forms of questioning) when done in the wrong place. Despite this, most Aztecs do own some of this equipment. They wear and use it whenever they safely can as a means of showing pride in their heritage.

QUETZALCOATL PRIEST

TRAITS & APTITUDES

Deftness 2d6
  Throwin': Aztec magic, balanced 4
Nimbleness 3d6
  Climbin' 1
  Sneak 1
Strength 1d6
Quickness 4d6
Vigor 2d6
Cognition 3d8
  Scrutinize 1
  Search 2
Knowledge 2d10
  Academia: occult, Aztec
    culture and lore 3
  Area knowledge
    (Mexico) 2
  Nahuatl 2
  Spanish 1
  Medicine (general) 2
Mien 3d8
  Overawe 2
Smarts 2d10
  Survival
    (mountains)
    1
Spirit 4d12
  Guts 2
Wind: 18
Edges:
  Arcane background:
    Aztec 3
  Good birth omens 3
Hindrances:
  Blood sacrifice -2
  Enemy (Secret Empire) -3
  Old Ways vow -3
  Superstitious -2
Special Abilities:
  Rituals 4: Fast, maim, scar
  Favors: Call weather (Tlaloc's
    blessing), healing (Patecatl's
    touch), lightning strike (Tlaloc's
    dart) turtle's shell
Gear: Feathered cloak, obsidian
  needles, tlauiztli, shield, 10 darts, 110
  pesos.

PERSONALITY

The gods must be fed with blood, but that blood need not come from human sacrifice. Each of us can give a little of ourselves each day instead. Is that so much to ask to keep the sun alive, to save the world from destruction by earthquakes?

The Lords of the Obsidian Blade and their sorcerers are not true priests. They are abominations which must be destroyed. Their plans to slaughter the whites are no better than those of Cortés, who massacred our people for gold and power. To repay cruelty with cruelty is not wisdom—it is folly.

Quote: "Feathered or not, this serpent has fangs."

Renegade Jaguar Knight

Traits & Aptitudes

Deftness 2d10
  Throwin': balanced, unbalanced 3
Nimbleness 2d12
  Climbin' 1
  Fightin': macahuitl, spear 4
  Sneak 2
Strength 2d10
Quickness 4d8
Vigor 3d8
Cognition 4d6
  Search 2
  Trackin' 2
Knowledge 3d6
  Area knowledge:
    Mexico 2
  Nahuatl 2
  English 1
  Spanish 1
Mien 2d6
  Overawe 2
Smarts 2d6
  Survival: mountains 2
Spirit 2d6
  Guts 2
Wind: 14
Edges:
  Good birth omens 3
Hindrances:
  Bloodthirsty –2
  Enemy: Secret
    Empire –5
  Vengeful –3
Gear: Two-handed
  macahuitl,
  obsidian-tipped
  spear, atlatl,
  tlauiztli,
  shield, 145
  pesos.

Personality

I have had enough of the Lords of the Obsidian Blade! Their magics, and the things they summon with them, are blights upon the land.

This is not what was intended. I am the noble son of a noble people, and I will only fight for what is just and right. The spirit of the jaguar lives within me, and I will obey its call, not the orders of the Lords.

Quote: "Here's an obsidian blade for you!"

THE
MARSHAL'S
HANDBOOK

CHAPTER FOUR: THE REST OF THE STORY

So, you want to run a *Deadlands* game in Mexico, eh? Well, whether you just want your posse to visit, or expect them to remain there full-time, here are a few tips to get you started.

JUST VISITIN'

Most Marshals will likely use Mexico as a new and interesting place for their posses to visit for an extended story arc of some sort. They may be sent there to track down bandits, help one side or the other in the ongoing civil war, kill critters, spy on the French Foreign Legion, or find out the secret of the Lords of the Obsidian Blade. There are plenty of ways to get your posse down there, Marshal. Some of them include:

THE EXPLORER'S SOCIETY

If you've got *Rascals, Varmints & Critters*, you've heard about the Explorer's Society. It's a group, with roots dating back to old England, that explores the Weird West looking for new and interesting trophies for their hunting lodge walls. That, at least, is their cover story, and while it's mostly true, it conceals a deeper, more benign purpose: monster hunting. The Explorers are well aware that the world's changed for the worse in the past 14 years, and they've taken it on themselves to investigate what's going on and polish off the nasties which the Reckoning has birthed.

Since there's no shortage of nasties in Mexico, an Explorer's Society expedition south of the border is the perfect excuse to get your posse down to Mexico. Hunting devil bats and Mojave rattlers gets old after awhile; going after coatls, tzitzimime, and other Mexican horrors may be a refreshing change of pace.

If at least one posse member doesn't belong to the Society, an Explorer may hire them as guides, guards, or "support" for his own expedition. That way they're guaranteed to make a few bucks for the adventure—assuming they survive.

CURRENT EVENTS

Muckraking characters may be attracted to Mexico to report on the civil war, or perhaps to follow an Explorer as he delves into the mysteries of the Mexican unknown. If a reporter were to get wind of the Secret Empire of the Aztecs, just imagine how fast he'd make tracks for Mexico. What journalist worth his salt could resist a story involving secret cults, political conspiracies, human sacrifice, and horrifying gods all rolled into one?

DIPLOMACY

Characters with political connections, or who've attracted the attention of the higher-ups in either the Confederate or Union government, may be assigned to lead a diplomatic embassy to one or more of the Powers That Be in Mexico. A state visit to the court of Emperor Maximillian would be relatively straightforward and out in the open, though it might involve court intrigue, dress balls, or other occasions for some heavy roleplaying.

Carrying a governmental message to Benito Juárez or Porfirio Díaz is another matter altogether. Since both men (and their followers) are technically rebels, neither the Confederacy nor the Union would want to visit them openly. However, a secret expedition might take place to enlist their support in exchange for money or future favors. For example, the Confederacy might want to persuade Juárez to attack Santa Anna's invading army from behind at the same time as the men in grey hit it head-on in southern California.

SPYING

The posse may be sent into Mexico to gauge the lay of the land, spy on the French Foreign Legion, or the like. Alternately, they might be hired to take a message to an undercover spy, or to retrieve sensitive information from one.

Missions like this are tailor-made for most posses. And, of course, there's always one complication—will the government they spied for try to eliminate them afterwards?

FOLLOWIN' THE BAD GUYS

Some posses may visit Mexico involuntarily. On the one hand, they might follow bandits, renegade Legionnaires, or some abomination across the border without knowing it. On the other, they might be taken prisoner by one of those groups and toted back home across someone's saddle. Either way, once they're in Mexico, the posse members may want to look around rather than heading straight for home—or they may have to work with one side or another in the civil war to get a way home.

SOUTH O' THE BORDER CAMPAIGNS

Some Marshals may want to base an entire campaign in Mexico. There's nothing wrong with this. In a lot of ways, Mexico isn't very different from the typical western environment of *Deadlands.* It has badlands, deserts, cowboys, mountain ranges, abominations, a civil war (albeit a three-way one), an evil conspiracy to take over the country, and abominations aplenty. However, there are some important differences to keep account of.

COWBOY IN THE JUNGLE

Mexico features some terrain that most *Deadlands* campaigns don't. First, it's got jungles. Your posse's going to have to go pretty far south to get to them, of course, but they'll probably end up there sooner or later. Most cowpokes aren't quite sure how to deal with rain forests, parrots, jaguars, and jungle abominations—it will take some getting used to.

Second, there are volcanoes. Mountains are one thing, but unless your posse's been hanging around

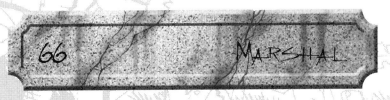

y

MARSHAL

certain parts of Oregon, volcanoes (and earthquakes) are likely to seem mighty terrifying to them. Think of this as a good tool to help you build feelings of horror or helplessness into your scenarios.

RACE AND CLASS

Race and class play a more important part of Mexican society than they do in most *Deadlands* settings. Characters who come from the upper classes will receive privileges which lower-class characters won't. *Campesinos* may not be allowed to go some places or do some things.

Class often governs which side a character supports in the civil war. Liberals and reformers tend to support Juárez, as do many in the lower classes. Older, richer traditionalists, on the other hand, will support whoever does the most to maintain their privileges and wealth and the power of the Catholic Church and the military—Díaz or Maximillian, they probably don't care provided they come out of things with their *haciendas* and lands intact. Mexicans hungry for power or advancement may toady to the Emperor or support Díaz, as do many Mexican patriots who can't stand Maximillian but are uncomfortable with Juárez's ideas about reform.

Similarly, women don't have as much freedom and equality as they do in most parts of the Weird West. In the *macho* Mexican society, they're expected to stay home, keep house, and remain quiet. The civil war has changed this a little, but not much. Playing a female character will be a roleplaying challenge.

CHARLES BASCOMB

If you'd like to use Charles Bascomb (and his extensive knowledge of goings-on south o' the border) in your campaign as an extra, just use the Huckster archetype in the *Weird West Player's Guide*, but increase his *dinero* to 5 and give him *belongings* 5 to represent his extensive property in the Confederacy. Also give him *area knowledge (Mexico)* 2 and *academia: Aztec culture and lore* 1.

VOLCANO TERRORS

Volcanoes are pretty frightening all by themselves, Brimstone Men or no—anything that can spew red-hot rock, boiling mud, and mountains of ash is something you ought to be careful around. The Secret Empire's well aware of this fact, and knows that it can use the volcanoes in the Valley of Mexico and elsewhere as weapons if it has to. The Lords of the Obsidian Blade have prepared a ritual which calls on Chantico, goddess of volcanic fire, and Tlaltecuhtli, the earth monster god, to make a particular volcano erupt.

It's not an easy ritual, though. To get it to work properly, the Secret Empire has to do several things. First, they have to choose the priests to perform this

ritual, and set them to performing regular daily sacrifices of their own blood in special ceremonies performed at an altar on the side of the volcano itself.

Second, they must obtain the materials for, and make, special sacrificial garb for the head priest and sacrificial victim to wear. The necessary materials include the pelts of the mysterious, and dangerous, cloud jaguars of the mountains of the Yucatan; feathers from the legendary *cacique veranero*, or firebird, which lives in and around Mexican volcanoes; and jade ornaments made of jade taken from Zapotec tombs (see below). Marshal, you can probably run several scenarios based around having the posse try to stop the Aztecs from getting their hands on this stuff if you want.

Finally, the ritual's last step, the action which sets the spell in motion, is a human sacrifice. The priests dress the sacrifice in sacred garb, take him to another altar near the top of the volcano in question, and rip his heart out. Once that's done, all the priests have to do is run like Mictlan to get to safety before their super-weapon blows.

After the ritual has been completed, it takes about an hour for the volcano to get itself really worked up. During this time, the surrounding area is shaken by tremors and poisonous gases and choking clouds of ash spew from the volcano's mouth and flow down its slopes.

OLMEC JADE FIGURINES

The Olmec jade axehead-figurines which Bascomb describes represent a ubiquitous creature in Olmec myth, the werejaguar. The exact significance of the werejaguar remains unknown. So, unfortunately for your posse, is the fact that these figurines are cursed. Anyone who owns one for long will slowly be

transformed into a werejaguar himself! At first the transformations only occur once a month or so, at night, when the victim thinks he has been sleeping. Gradually they occur more and more frequently, until, after about eight months, the victim becomes a werejaguar permanently. Werejaguars were sacred to the Olmecs, but in these post-Reckoning days, they are just another tool of the Reckoners.

PROFILE: OLMEC WEREJAGUAR

Corporeal: D:3d10, N:4d10, S:3d8, Q:4d6, V:3d10

Climbin' 4d10, dodge 4d10, fightin': claws 5d10, sneak 6d10

Mental: C:3d6, K:3d6, M:4d6, Sm:3d6, Sp:3d6

Overawe 4d6

Pace: 10

Size: 6

Wind: 16

Terror: 6

Special Abilities:

　Armor: 1

　Claws: STR+2d6

　Fangs: STR+1d6

　Leap: A werejaguar can leap up to 30 feet.

Description: In its human form, a werejaguar has a fat, almost babyish face with an odd crease down the center of its head and a harelip or cleft palate-like deformity of its mouth (which it may try to hide with a moustache).

OLMEC GIANT HEADS

There's nothing sinister or dangerous about the gigantic Olmec stone heads (unless perhaps a posse member somehow manages to cause one to fall on himself). However, posse members who visit the Gulf Coast of Mexico are certain to become suspicious about them. So, feel free to concoct some local legends about how the heads were consecrated with human sacrifices (so that ghosts now haunt them), that the heads cover up the entrances to Olmec tombs filled with golden treasure, and so forth—whatever will yank your posse's chain the hardest.

THE BAT GOD

While most of the Zapotec gods and myths are pure fiction, one of them—the greatly feared Bat God—has a basis in fact. Posse members who go poking around too much in the subterranean tombs of Monte Albán may have the misfortune to disturb his place of slumber and release him into the world once more.

The Bat God is an enormous devil bat which the Zapotecs worshipped and propitiated with human sacrifice and many valuable objects. For centuries it has slept in a cavern deep beneath a hill marked only by the ruins of a great temple the Zapotecs built to honor it. If anyone digs through the rubble of the temple and finds the long-hidden doorway into the bat's lair, it awakens and attacks.

Characters who manage to release and kill the Bat God can recover several hundred dollars' worth of gold and jade artifacts from its "tomb." The artifacts are worth much more if preserved and sold to museums and collectors, but that takes longer than melting them down and requires a lot of travel or correspondence with various curators.

For basic information about devil bats, see the *Marshal's Handbook*.

PROFILE: THE BAT GOD

Corporeal: D:4d12, N:4d12, S:3d12+4, Q:4d12, V:4d10
Dodge 5d12, fightin': claws 6d12, sneak 3d12 (7d12 from the air)
Mental: C:4d12, K:2d6, M:4d12, Sm:3d8, Sp:3d8
Overawe 6d12
Pace: 4 running/36 flying
Size: 9
Wind: 25
Terror: 13
Special Abilities:
　Claws: STR+2d6
　Flying: Pace 36
　Screech: Once per round the bat god can utter an ear piercing screech. Anyone within 10 yards of the creature must make a *Vigor* roll against an Onerous (7) TN or be stunned.
　Weakness: Noise Sensitivity (as regular devil bat)

Description: A gigantic devil bat. The membranes of the bat's ears and wings are tinged a deep, blood red.

LA NOCHE TRISTE

The Spaniards who died on *La Noche Triste* because they carried too much stolen Aztec gold have not rested easily. Although much of the lake has been filled in and paved over by now, occasionally some of them return from the dead and claw their way up to the surface. Then they stalk the living, trying to sate their dual lust for brains and gold. Anyone they catch is killed, eaten, and stripped bare of anything valuable. The Triste Dead have the ability to "smell" gold, so they can easily find the best victims.

PROFILE: TRISTE DEAD

Corporeal: D:3d6, N:3d8, S:3d10, Q:2d6, V:3d8

Climbin' 1d8, dodge 2d8, fightin': brawlin', saber 2d8, horse ridin' 2d8, shootin': rifle 2d6

Mental: C:3d8, K:1d6, M:2d6, Sm:1d6, Sp:1d4

Artillery: cannons 1d8, overawe 5d6

Pace: 8

Size: 6

Wind: N/A

Terror: 9

Special Abilities:

Bite: STR

Armor: The Triste Dead wear rusty 16th century Spanish breastplates and helmets. This provides them with Armor 1.

Gold Sense: Triste Dead can detect large quantities of gold (anything more than a ring or two) within 100 feet. They carry bags and pouches of gold with them (though some of the containers have rotted or burst, spilling their contents into the mud beneath Mexico City). Anyone who destroys one is certainly entitled to claim this booty for himself. (A fiendish Marshal may place an ancient Aztec curse on the stolen gold, however.) If a victim drops his gold, the undead soldier takes it and leaves in search of another victim.

Weapons: Many Triste Dead carry rusty swords (treat as if it was a saber). They also know how to use weapons like rifles and cannons, but their knowledge applies to weapons over three centuries old, so apply a -2 penalty to any roll with those Aptitudes.

Undead.

Description: A skeletal body wearing rusty 350-year-old Spanish armor, carrying bags and pouches which either hold Aztec gold, or have burst and are empty. Many carry rusty sabers or rotted, non-functional muskets

ITURBIDE

The official histories don't tell you what happened *after* Augustín Iturbide was executed. His body was turned over to his family for burial. They sealed it away in the family mausoleum, and everyone soon forgot about Mexico's first emperor.

Everyone, that is, but the Secret Empire. Sensing a tool they could use, the Aztec sorcerers "awakened" Iturbide after the Reckoning. Confused by his long "sleep," Iturbide doesn't realize he's dead (you'd think the fact that he's not much more than a skeleton wearing a tattered military uniform full of bullet holes would clue him in), and still thinks he can reclaim the "throne" of Mexico. However, first he wants to satisfy his thirst for vengeance against Santa Anna.

He hates the general with every fiber of his undead heart, and would like nothing better than to rip him limb from limb. Since returning Harrowed, he has been stalking Santa Anna, hoping to catch him alone. Unfortunately, he moves much more slowly than the general, so he's constantly trailing after him and his army, spreading terror as he walks.

PROFILE: ITURBIDE

Corporeal: D:4d8, N:3d10, S:4d12, Q:3d8, V:3d8

Climbin' 1d10, dodge 3d10, fightin': brawlin', sword 4d10, horse ridin' 3d10, shootin': pistol, rifle 4d10

Mental: C:2d8, K:3d6, M:3d8, Sm:2d6, Sp:2d8

Academia: Mexican history 3d6, academia: military theory 2d6, artillery: cannons 3d8, leadership 3d8, overawe 4d8, trackin' 4d8

Pace: 10

Wind: 24

Dominion: Harrowed 2, manitou 6

Harrowed Powers: Arcane protection 2, marked for death 3

Edges: Level-headed 5, "the stare" 1, tough as nails 4

Hindrances: Aura o' death -4, degeneration -5 (Terror 9), yearnin' (kill Santa Anna and reclaim rule of Mexico) -5

Gear: Tattered uniform, saber.

EMPEROR MAXIMILLIAN

Bascomb's analysis of Emperor Maximillian is a pretty accurate one for someone who's never even talked to the man. Although aristocratic, and sometimes haughty, Maximillian tries to be a good ruler with his peoples' best interests at heart. He could be a saint, though, and the Mexicans still wouldn't like him. Whatever good he may do can never balance against their perception of him as a puppet ruler foisted off on them by a foreign invader. The Mexicans were never crazy about the French before they invaded their country, and they haven't done much to make friends since then.

Due to the time it takes to get messages back and forth to Mexico from France, Emperor Maximillian is largely independent of his patron Napoleon III. However, the one thing he absolutely depends on the French ruler for is military support. Half of his army is French (or at least French-recruited), and without them his regime would collapse in the face of attacks from the rebels Juárez and Díaz.

Emperor Maximillian has reasonable trust in Santa Anna, since he knows the general's interests are closely tied to his own, but he watches him carefully to make sure he obeys orders without twisting them for his benefit. He does not trust Santa Anna's advisor Xitlan at all, though, and is considering ordering Santa Anna to dispose of him—this could be dangerous for Maximillian..

EMPRESS CARLOTA

The Empress has always been a little, shall we say, "high strung." Lately, though, she's taken a turn for the worse. For the past several months, Carlota's been certifiably insane.

A few months ago, while gazing absentmindedly out the window during one of her parties, Carlota happened to see an Aztec sorcerer, accompanied by a *thing*, slinking through the shadows. The scene transfixed her and unhinged her mind. She became convinced it was all part of some elaborate plot to "get" her. Since then she's become suspicious and paranoid of just about everyone and everything, especially anything to do

with Indians (including Aztecs). She won't eat anything until one of her servants tastes it first. She refuses to be the first person to enter a room. She believes stories of ghosts, monsters, and mystics, and has consulted several astrologers and other such folk for advice. She hides her lunacy well, though; no one, not even her husband, thinks anything of her behavior except to write it off to her "moody" nature.

The truth is, her suspicions are, in some small part, correct. While no one intends her any harm directly, she has glimpsed something of the truth behind the Reckoning, even though she cannot articulate it, and the Reckoners know it. When the Lords of the Obsidian Blade rise up to take back what is theirs, she will be one of the first people sacrificed to Tezcatlipoca.

THE MINISTER OF WAR

Unknown to either the Emperor or anyone else on the Council, Osvaldo Guttierez-Arias is actually almost half-Aztec. He despises the Spanish half of his heritage, for all he wears it proudly in public.

Guttierez-Arias is a pawn of the Lords of the Obsidian Blade, whom he practically worships. He is aware of the nature and scope of their plot, but few of the details, which he would never reveal. He plays the part of fop, while secretly working to overthrow the government that has elevated him to such power.

Despite his dandified habits, the Minister has had military experience and is a skilled fencer. Anyone who insults or challenges him is sure to have a fight on his hands. Nor is he above cheating if he feels he can do so without getting caught. He takes a fiendish pleasure in that moment when the opponent realizes he never had a chance. He particularly likes using a colorless poison on his blade which causes paralysis. Anyone taking as little as 1 point of Wind damage from the blade must make a Hard (9) *Vigor* roll or be paralyzed for 1d4 actions. A paralyzed victim cannot defend himself.

Guttierez-Arias has had his eye on the Empress for some time. When the Secret Empire rises up and takes over Mexico, he plans to "enjoy" her before turning her over to the priests for sacrifice.

MINISTER FLORES Y MACEDA

Jesús Flores y Maceda serves Emperor Maximillian as a troubleshooter and spy. These days he spends a lot of time scouting out rebel forces or keeping close tabs on Santa Anna in California. He uses a special steam wagon to get around quickly.

Flores y Maceda has begun to develop suspicions about Santa Anna's advisor, Xitlan. However, as yet they're just that — vague suspicions. He doesn't have any evidence that Xitlan is up to anything criminal, or if he is, what exactly it might be. But he's trying to learn more.

MINISTER BALTHAZAR

The Justice Minister is as corrupt and venal as they come. He'll let anyone out of jail, or sic his men on anyone, if the price is right. However, he doesn't want to lose his position, so he makes sure to keep his illegal activities as secret as possible. He's amassed quite a fortune since Maximillian arrived, and he plans to go right on making himself richer. If anyone ever tumbles to his schemes, he's set up several escape routes that allow him to get to Veracruz, where a fast ship will take him to Spain or some Caribbean island.

The Emperor does not suspect his old friend of any criminal activity. He has no plans to remove Balthazar from office.

PROFILE: MINISTER JESUS FLORES Y MACEDA

Corporeal: D:3d8, N:4d10, S:4d8, Q:3d10, V:2d8

Climbin' 2d8, dodge 4d8, drivin': steam wagon 3d10, fightin': brawlin' 4d10, horse ridin' 1d10, shootin': pistol, rifle 4d10, throwin': balanced 3d8

Mental: C:3d12, K:4d6, M:3d8, Sm:3d8, Sp:2d6

Area knowledge (Mexico, southern California) 3d6, artillery: cannons 1d12, bluff 4d8, disguise 3d6, gamblin' 3d8, guts 3d6, French 1d6, Spanish 2d6, leadership 2d8, overawe 4d8, persuasion 2d8, scrutinize 3d12, search 3d12, streetwise 3d8, survival: desert 4d8, trackin' 3d12

Pace: 10

Wind: 14

Edges: Belongin's (steam wagon) 4, level headed 5, nerves o' steel 1, social class: peninsulare 3

Hindrances: Cautious -3, curious -3, intolerance (Texans) -1, vengeful -3

Gear: Winchester '73, double-action Colt Peacemaker, 50 rounds of ammunition for both guns, knife, rope, steam wagon, two weeks' rations, 128 pesos, $78 Union, $157 Confederate

MIGUEL VASQUEZ-TRUJILLO

Far from being loyal to Benito Juárez, Vasquez-Trujillo is the Emperor's man through and through. In fact, he's part of an elaborate plot which Minister of Justice Balthazar and some of his Rurales cooked up. The idea is to attract the attention of Juárez or his people by seeming to support their aims in the Chamber of Deputies. After being taken into their confidence, Vasquez-Trujillo will reveal everything he learns about them to Minister Balthazar—all in exchange for personal favors and money from the Minister, of course.

Juárez and his men have been keeping a close eye on Vasquez-Trujillo, but so far they have not contacted him. Juárez is suspicious of Vasquez-Trujillo's motives, but he has no hard evidence to back up his gut feelings. He plans to contact the deputy soon unless information incriminating Vasquez-Trujillo arises.

THE RURALES

Unlike the Texas Rangers, the Rurales don't know much about the Reckoning and are not specifically charged with stopping abominations. Of course, many Rurales have encountered abominations on their patrols, and they realize that strange things now walk the Earth, but they have not figured out when this happened or why. The Aztec conspirators close to the Emperor and other high Mexican officials have used their influence to discourage any Rurales who want to investigate further.

A Rurale typically wears a large Mexican hat, a decorated jacket, and black pants with silver ornaments along the sides. He carries a rifle, a large pistol, and a sword. Marshals who want to use the Rurales as antagonists for their posses can use the following character profile to represent the typical Rurale. Players who want to create Rurales should take a look in Chapter Two.

PROFILE: TYPICAL RURALE

Corporeal: D:3d8, N:3d8, S:3d6, Q:2d6, V:2d6

Climbin' 1d8, dodge 2d8, fightin': brawlin', saber 3d8, horse ridin' 2d8, quick draw: pistol 3d6, shootin': pistol, rifle 3d8, sneak 3d8

Mental: C:2d6, K:2d6, M:2d8, Sm:3d6, Sp:2d6

Area knowledge (Mexico) 4d6, guts 2d6, Spanish 2d6, overawe 2d8, scrutinize 2d6, search 3d6, streetwise 3d6, survival: desert 3d6, trackin' 2d6

Pace: 8

Wind: 16

Edges: Law man 4, nerves o' steel 1, social class: mestizo 1, tough as nails 2

Hindrances: Intolerance (Texans) -3, obligation (enforce the law in all of Mexico) -1, vengeful -3

Gear: Pistol (varying types), rifle (varying types), ammunition for both guns, saber, horse, badge

MARSHAL ACHILLE BAZAIN

Achille Bazain dresses like a court dandy, but underneath he's made of iron and vinegar. Although he's over 60 and has spent much of his life in the field leading troops, the Marshal has barely slowed down. He brooks no disrespect or disobedience and doesn't give ground before anyone except the two Emperors, Maximillian and Napoleon III. Although they fear him, his troops love him, and most would follow him into Hell and back if he asked them to.

Bazain has learned fluent Spanish during his time in Mexico, and some (including, perhaps, Napoleon III) suspect that he has ambitions to rule Mexico. If

so, Maximillian seems unaware of it; he places complete trust in the Marshal.

Bazain's biggest soft spot is his devotion to his young wife, Soledad, whom he left back in France. Although he has mistresses—he wouldn't be a Frenchman if he didn't—he seems to love only her. A Spaniard twenty years younger than he, Soledad is a pretty little flirt who nevertheless seems as devoted to her husband as he is to her. Bazaine longs for the day when he feels Mexico is safe enough to bring her there; for now, he must content himself with writing her letters.

PROFILE: MARSHAL ACHILLE BAZAIN

Corporeal: D:3d8, N:2d10, S:2d6, Q:3d6, V:2d6

Dodge 2d10, fightin': brawlin', saber 4d10, horse ridin' 2d10, shootin': pistol, rifle 5d8, swimmin' 2d10

Mental: C:3d8, K:3d6, M:4d10, Sm:3d6, Sp:2d6

Academia: Military Theory 5d8, area knowledge (France) 3d6, area knowledge (Mexico) 2d6, artillery: cannons 4d10, guts 3d6, French 2d6, Spanish 2d6, leadership 5d10, overawe 5d10, persuasion 3d10, scrutinize 3d10, search 3d10

Pace: 10

Wind: 12

Edges: Brave 2, eagle eyes 1, rank (Marshal), "the stare" 1, "the voice" (threatening) 1

Hindrances: Ferner –3, intolerance (Mexicans) –3, obligation (obey the Emperor(s)) –5

Gear: Chassepot, exceptional horse (brave, smart), saber, .38 Navy pistol, 20 .38 rounds, dress uniform

BAZAIN'S BODYGUARDS

Because Mexicans hate him so much, Bazain has two bodyguards which accompany him everywhere except into his mistress's boudoir (at least as far as he knows. One is Corporal duMont, a veteran of the French Foreign Legion. DuMont's got the scars to prove he's been in plenty of fights, and his skin has the sunburned, rawhide look of a man who's used to tthe out-of-doors.

The other bodyguard is an Indian who goes by the name of "Juan." Bazain chose him not only for his intimidating size and demeanor, but because he speaks both Spanish and Indian languages and can figure out what the natives are saying behind the Marshal's back. He also helps the Marshal keep an eye on Santa Anna's native advisor, Xitlan—or so Bazain thinks. In fact, Juan is actually 8 Rabbit, an Aztec warrior devoted to the cause of the Lords of the Obsidian Blade. He spies on Bazain for the Lords, and passes his "master" false information about Xitlan's plans and activities.

Profile: Corporal Dumont

Corporeal: D:3d12, N:3d10, S:4d8, Q:3d8, V:2d8

Climbin' 4d10, dodge 3d12, fightin': brawlin', knife, saber 5d10, horse ridin' 3d10, shootin': pistol, rifle 4d12, sneak 3d10

Mental: C:2d6, K:2d6, M:1d8, Sm:2d6, Sp:1d8

Academia: Military Theory 2d6, area knowledge (Mexico) 2d6, artillery: cannons 2d6, guts 2d8, French 1d6, German 2d6, Spanish 1d6, overawe 5d10, scrutinize 2d6, search 2d6, streetwise 4d6, survival: desert, mountains 3d6

Pace: 10

Wind: 22

Edges: Level headed 5, sand 2, tough as nails 3

Hindrances: Ferner –3, intolerance (Mexicans) –3, obligation (protect the Marshal) –4

Gear: Chassepot, horse, uniform, large knife

Profile: "Juan" (8 Rabbit)

Corporeal: D:2d10, N:3d12, S:4d8, Q:3d8, V:2d6

Bow 2d10, climbin' 3d12, dodge 3d10, fightin': brawlin', knife, macahuitl 6d12, horse ridin' 2d12, shootin': pistol 2d10, swimmin' 3d10, sneak 5d12

Mental: C:3d6, K:2d6, M:4d8, Sm:2d6, Sp:2d6

Area knowledge (Mexico) 4d6, guts 4d6, Spanish 1d6, Nahuatl 2d6, Zapotec 1d6, overawe 4d8, search 3d6, survival: desert, mountains 4d6

Pace: 12

Wind: 22

Edges: Big ears 1, brawny 3, the stare 1, thick-skinned 3, tough as nails 5

Hindrances: Bloodthirsty –2, intolerance (non-Aztecs) –3, oath (bring Lords of Obsidian Blade to power) –5, superstitious (follows Aztec superstitions) –2

Gear: Chassepot, macahuitl, *ichcauipilli* armor, horse, large knife

Colonel Castelnau

Philippe Castelnau is Napoleon III's trump card in case Bazain comes down with a case of adventurism. The French Emperor has maintained a secret communication with Castelnau as a way of watching over Bazain. Should Bazain decide to try to take Mexico for himself, Castelnau is prepared to move against him.

Castelnau has a small group of soldiers among the garrison at the Imperial Palace who are personally loyal to him.

Corporal Willette

Unknown to Marshal Bazain, the ever-efficient Corporal Willette has loyalties other than to France. Specifically, he is a level-eight initiate of the Royal Court, a secretive group of hucksters devoted to serving the Reckoners (see *Hucksters & Hexes,* for more information, Marshal). The Court worries about possible Mexican attacks on the Confederacy (primarily on Texas and New Orleans), and arranged to insert Willette into Bazain's inner circle to gather information on French and Mexican intentions.

Willette suspects that "Juan" is not all he appears to be, and he's definitely suspicious of Xitlan. However, he hasn't investigated these matters closely yet, since he's too busy with his cover job and his primary mission for the Court.

PROFILE: CORPORAL WILLETTE

Corporeal: D:4d8, N:3d8, S:3d6, Q:4d8, V:3d6

Climbin' 1d8, dodge 2d8, fightin': brawlin' 3d8, horse ridin' 2d8, quick draw: pistol 2d8, shootin': pistol 3d8, sleight o' hand 2d8, sneak 3d8

Mental: C:3d10, K:2d10, M:2d12, Sm:2d10, Sp:3d8

Academia: Military Theory 1d10, academia: occult 3d10, area knowledge (Weird West) 2d10, bluff 3d10, gamblin' 3d10, English 2d10, French 1d10, Spanish 1d10

Pace: 8

Wind: 14

Edges: Arcane Background: Huckster 3, keen 3, thick-skinned 3

Hindrances: Cautious –3, greedy –2, randy –3

Special Abilities:

Hexslingin' 5

Hexes: Corporeal twist, helpin' hand, hunch, phantom fingers, private eye, soul blast, trinkets

Gear: Chassepot, Remington Double Derringer of quality, 10 rounds of ammunition, uniform, one copy of *Hoyle's Book Of Games*

LA LEGION ETRANGERE

In case you want to throw your posse up against a squad of Legionnaires, you can use the character profile for the Legionnaire on page 52. If they aren't enough of a match for your posse, here's what a typical *experienced* member of the Legion looks like. The thing they're most noted for is their toughness; a Legionnaire doesn't surrender, and he never just lays down and dies—you've got to shoot him four or five times before he'll give up the ghost.

The standard Legionnaire uniform is a blue greatcoat, with the skirts usually buttoned back for marching, a red and blue *kepi* (brimmed cap) with a white *puggaree* (headcloth) dangling from behind to keep the sun off the head, and various items of kit. However, in Mexico, many Legionnaires adopt more Mexican garb, abandoning the greatcoat and exchanging the *kepi* for a broad-brimmed Mexican hat.

PROFILE: EXPERIENCED LEGIONNAIRE

Corporeal: D:3d8, N:3d8, S:3d6, Q:2d6, V:4d6

Climbin' 2d8, dodge 4d8, fightin': brawlin', knife, saber 4d8, shootin': rifle, pistol, shotgun 5d8, sneak 3d8

Mental: C:3d6, K:2d6, M:2d6, Sm:2d6, Sp:2d6

Academia: military theory 2d6, artillery: cannons 2d6, gamblin' 1d6, guts 4d6, French 1d6, native language (Marshal's choice) 2d6, overawe 3d6, scrutinize 2d6, search 3d6, streetwise 2d6, survival: desert 3d6, one academia, professional, or trade Aptitude (Marshal's choice; represents former profession) at level 2

Pace: 8

Wind: 14

Edges: Brave 2, sand 3, tough as nails 1

Hindrances: Ferner –3, intolerance (non-Legionnaires) –3, obligation (serve the Legion, protect France) –4

Gear: Chassepot, uniform, large knife or saber.

THE DESERTER

The story Bascomb heard about the man who was brought back to Mexico and executed ten years after he deserted the Legion is true. The Legion refuses to let any deserter get away with his crime if it can help it, and only one penalty—death—awaits those who think they can leave the Legion behind.

But in *Deadlands,* of course, death ain't necessarily a permanent thing. It certainly wasn't in this case. The deserter, a German named Karl Katau, didn't much like the idea of being dragged away from his home and being shot. The Reckoners took advantage of his thirst for vengeance and desire to return home and brought him back Harrowed. Now he's got two goals: first, slaughter any Legionnaire who was part of the firing squad which killed him; two, get back home. After he tracks down and offs his killers, he'll start the long trek back to St. Louis. And, of course, as long as he's in Mexico, he'll also encourage other Legionnaires to desert, and even help them do it—if they don't run at the sight of him.

Unfortunately, the Deserter won't get a very good reception if he ever makes it back home. While he was still lying out in the desert, coyotes and vultures bit off several pieces of him, so he doesn't exactly look like himself. In fact, just about anyone who gets a good look at the Deserter has to make a Fair (5) *guts* check to keep from losing his lunch.

Profile: The Deserter

Corporeal: D:4d6, N:2d10, S:3d10, Q:2d8, V:3d6

Climbin' 1d10, dodge 3d10, fightin': brawlin', knife, saber 4d10, shootin': rifle 3d10, sneak 1d10

Mental: C:2d6, K:2d6, M:4d10, Sm:2d6, Sp:2d8

Academia: military theory 1d6, artillery: cannons 1d6, gamblin' 1d6, guts 3d8, French 1d6, German 2d6, overawe 3d10, scrutinize 2d6, search 2d6, survival: desert 3d6, trade: carpentry 2d6

Pace: 10

Wind: 14

Dominion: Harrowed 4, manitou 4

Harrowed Powers: Unholy reflexes 3, voice o' the damned 2

Edges: Brawny 3, fleet-footed 2, the stare 1, the voice (threatening) 1

Hindrances: Degeneration -4, grim servant o' death -5, mean as a rattler -2, vengeful -3, yearnin' (kill firing squad; get home; protect deserters) -3

Gear: Mismatched clothes, knife, saber.

The Napoleon Of The West

Santa Anna is as described in the main text—a tough, intelligent (yet slightly mad) opponent. He might not be able to stand up to your posse's best gunslinger on the streets of Laredo, but he knows damn well what battlefields to pick and when to fight, so it's not likely that gunslinger will ever have a chance to slap leather with him anyhow.

Santa Anna desperately wants to recover his artificial leg. He doesn't know why, or where it is, except that it's somewhere in Texas. See below for more information on this eerie limb.

Even more than that, though, Santa Anna wants to recover the glory he once had. He wants to be back in the "President's" seat, ruling over a Mexico expanded to her former borders. Convincing Maximillian to give him an army was just the first step. Now he has to increase that army (partly by achieving a grand victory in California), invade and conquer Texas, and then depose Maximillian and kick the French out of Mexico for good. He's not quite sure how he's going to do all that, but he's determined to try—and he'd accept help from anyone, even the Reckoners, to succeed.

Santa Anna and Baron LaCroix

One of the devil's bargains Santa Anna has made is with Baron Simone LaCroix, the head of the Bayou Vermillion railroad and master of the darkest voodoo magics. Santa Anna believes that Xitlan's powers come from the Baron somehow, and he initially raised the subject of an alliance with LaCroix in the hopes of "cutting out the middleman" and learning how to create zombie soldiers himself.

He hasn't gotten anywhere with that, of course, but he soon realized that the Baron could be a valuable ally in his own right, regardless of whether he can create walkin' dead or not. The Bayou Vermillion railroad runs right through southern Texas and along the border between the Confederacy and Mexico. As such, it's ideally suited to transporting Santa Anna's troops and supplies once he invades Texas.

He worked out an arrangement with the Baron in which he agreed not to damage any Bayou Vermillion property in exchange for the railroad's exclusive services supporting his army when the time comes. Of course, he'll still have to pay the Baron for these services, and LaCroix insists on carrying most of them out in secret to keep everyone from branding him a traitor, but the deal looks like it could turn out to be a good one for both parties.

Since coming to this arrangement, the Baron and the General have become close allies. Santa Anna has secretly visited LaCroix in New Orleans to invest in some of the Baron's businesses and seek his help in a potential coup against Maximillian—help LaCroix agreed to give. LaCroix has provided Santa Anna with several special walkin' dead to act as "commanders" in the General's undead army.

Xitlan, needless to say, doesn't like the increasing ties between Santa Anna and LaCroix. He rightly views them as a threat to his own influence and power.

Accordingly, he's turned the might of the Secret Empire against the interests of Bayou Vermillion. Whenever possible, Aztec warriors kidnap and sacrifice Bayou Vermillion employees, attack the Baron's trains, and damage Vermillion tracks and equipment. They don't often get the opportunity to do this, of course, but Xitlan is confident the Baron will extend himself too far sooner or later, allowing the Lords of the Obsidian Blade to dispose of him once and for all.

Santa Anna's Leg

You guessed it—Santa Anna's leg is a relic. A quick recap: At the Battle of Cerro Gordo, US forces surprised the Mexicans. Santa Anna was forced to flee the battlefield, leaving behind $18,000 in gold, his roasted chicken lunch, and his artificial leg. This prosthetic was made for the general after he lost his limb at Veracruz. The leather-covered, cork leg was constructed by cabinetmaker Charles Bartlett of New York City for $1300.

The leg was captured by a regiment from Illinois and taken as a war trophy. It ended up returning to Illinois with the troopers and now sits under glass in a Springfield museum—or so the US government would have people believe.

The leg on public display is a replica. The true leg is under lock-and-key in the Agency's Chicago headquarters. Agency hucksters who had come in contact with it realized that it had manifested arcane powers, but these have not yet been studied by Agency researchers, who feel that it is a minor relic at best.

In truth, the leg, which has become an embodiment of the hatred between Texans and Mexicans is potentially very powerful, especially if its original owner gets a hold of it. Santa Anna doesn't know this, but he can feel a subconscious pull from the relic which has made him determined to recover it.

Power: Santa Anna's leg has a number of powers. First, it melds with the body of anyone who straps it on, functioning as a normal leg. If the poor sod who put it on is not actually missing a leg (it straps on just above the knee), his original limb withers, blackens, and falls off over the course

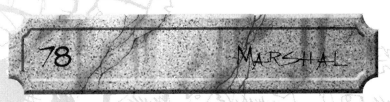

MARSHAL

of a week. The only way to stop this is for a *blessed* character to perform a successful *exorcism* on the limb. Once attached, it can be removed with an *exorcism* or a good bone saw. Anyone wearing the leg gains the *fleet-footed* Edge and gets a +4 bonus to all *leadership, overawe,* and *persuasion* rolls.

Secondly, any army carrying the leg (or commanded by a general wearing it), cannot be defeated by any force commanded by General Santa Anna.

Lastly, if Santa Anna regains his leg, it grants him an immunity to physical weapons. The only weapons which can harm him are the muskets of the Illinois regiment which captured his leg.

Taint: For Santa Anna, none. Anyone else who uses any of the leg's powers acquires a *yearnin'* to invade and conquer Texas.

Mexican Soldiers

Here's the other half of the Mexican military picture: the homegrown *soldado Mejicano.*

Thanks to Maximillian's money, Mexican soldiers are equipped with good American rifles, such as Winchesters or Spencer carbines. The Mexican cavalry also carry spear-like lances (use the spear statistics from *The Weird West Player's Guide*). When used from horseback, add +2 to the damage for every 5 yards the rider moved toward the target in the current round.

Their uniforms tend to be elaborate and gaudy, with different color patterns denoting particular battalions, companies, or squads.

Profile: Mexican Soldier

Corporeal: D:2d8, N:2d8, S:3d6, Q:2d6, V:4d6

Climbin' 1d8, dodge 1d8, fightin': brawlin', lance, saber 3d8, horse ridin' 2d8, shootin': pistol, rifle 3d8

Mental: C:2d6, K:2d6, M:3d6, Sm:2d6, Sp:2d6

Academia: military theory 1d6, Spanish 2d6, search 2d6, survival: desert 3d6

Pace: 8

Wind: 14

Edges: Fuero 3, social class: mestizo 3, tough as nails 1

Hindrances: Intolerance (Texans) –3, obligation (serve Santa Anna and Mexico) –4

Gear: Rifle, lance, uniform, horse, backpack

El Ejército de los Muertos

As described in *The Marshal's Handbook*, Santa Anna does indeed have an entire zombie army, raised and commanded by Xitlan, at his beck and call. When they can't get enough brains to eat, they're fed a mixture of meat and *plantagrito*, a special herb grown near Teotihuacan by the Lords of the Obsidian Blade (see *The Great Maze*, and elsewhere in this book, for details on this subject).

In addition to his basic undead soldiers, Santa Anna has a few "special" types. First, he has a corps of zombie cavalrymen riding undead horses; he uses them for lightning-quick raids under cover of darkness. Second, Baron LeCroix created for him a dozen or so "officer zombies" which lead some of the *Ejército*'s squads.

PROFILE: SOLDADO MUERTO

Corporeal: D:3d8, N:2d8, S:2d10, Q:3d10, V:2d8

Climbin' 2d8, dodge 3d8, fightin': brawlin', lance, saber 3d8, horse ridin' 4d8, shootin': carbine, pistol 4d8

Mental: C:2d10, K:1d6, M:1d6, Sm:1d6, Sp:1d4

Overawe 5d6, ridicule 1d6, search 3d10

Pace: 8

Size: 6

Wind: N/A

Terror: 9

Special Abilities:
  Bite: STR
  Weapons: *Soldados muertos* carry carbines, sabers, and lances.
  Undead.

Description: An undead soldier, wearing a tattered uniform of some kind and carrying weapons.

PROFILE: UNDEAD HORSE

Corporeal: D:2d4, N:2d12, S:3d10, Q:1d8, V:1d10

Fightin': brawlin' 2d12, swimmin' 3d12

Mental: C:1d6, K:1d6, M:2d8, Sm:1d6, Sp:1d4

Overawe 4d8

Pace: 24

Size: 10

Terror: 7

Special Abilities:
  Bite: STR

Description: A zombified horse. Some are pickled, some dry as a bone. All of them are disgusting at best, terrifying at worst. The eyes of these beasts glow a dark, sullen red.

PROFILE: OFICIAL MUERTO

Corporeal: D:3d8, N:3d8, S:3d10, Q:3d10, V:2d8

Climbin' 2d8, dodge 3d8, fightin': brawlin', lance, saber 4d8, horse ridin' 5d8, shootin': carbine 5d8

Mental: C:2d10, K:2d6, M:2d8, Sm:1d6, Sp:1d4

Overawe 5d8, search 3d10

Pace: 8

Size: 7

Wind: N/A

Terror: 9

Special Abilities:
  Bite: STR
  Corruption: If an *oficial muerto* makes a successful *fightin': brawlin'* attack against a living target, he can inflict the corruption of death upon that person. The corruption does 1d12 damage to the gizzard the round in which the victim is touched. Each round thereafter it does 1d4 damage to the gizzard until the victim dies, is doused with holy water, or a blessed character *lays on hands* on him.
  Weapons: *Oficiales muertos* carry pistols, sabers, and lances.
  Undead.

Description: As *soldado muerto*.

ANCHORS AWEIGH

Marshal, you can get the lowdown on the Mexican Armada, and its commander Grand Admiral Rodrigo Cobo, in *The Great Maze*. That book also has plenty of ships described for you in loving detail.

BENITO JUÁREZ

Bascomb's analysis of Juárez is dead-on accurate: he's the only hero in Mexico these days. He's not a foreign invader, like Maximillian and his French soldiers; he's not a potential demagogue harboring dreams of revenge, like the oft-deposed Santa Anna; and he's not seeking power for its own sake, like Díaz. He's just a man who has a vision of equal treatment for everyone, high and low alike, in a modern, democratic Mexico, and who's tired of seeing his countrymen trod on by foreigners, the

wealthy, and other exploiters. In short, this is the man your posse ought to be working for, if they've got hearts in their bodies and sense in their skulls.

His popularity's definitely his biggest asset, though. He doesn't have much in the way of a military force. Still, between that, his fighting skills (developed through years in the field) and his political savvy, he may just come out on top of this scrap—perhaps with a little help from some "independent regulators," from north of the border.

PROFILE: BENITO JUÁREZ

Corporeal: D:3d8, N:2d8, S:3d6, Q:2d8, V:2d6

Climbin' 1d8, dodge 2d8, horse ridin' 2d8, shootin': pistol, rifle 3d8, sneak 3d8

Mental: C:3d8, K:3d8, M:3d8, Sm:4d6, Sp:3d8

Academia: Mexican history and politics 5d8, area knowledge (Mexico) 3d8, guts 2d8, English 1d6, Spanish 2d6, Zapotec 1d6, leadership 4d8, overawe 3d8, persuasion 5d8, professional: lawyer 3d8, scroungin' 5d6, scrutinize 3d8, search 2d8, survival: desert, mountains 5d8, trackin' 4d8

Pace: 8
Wind: 14
Edges: Friends in high places (various friends and supporters all over Mexico) 5, renown 5
Hindrances: Enemy (the French; Santa Anna) -5, heroic -3, social class: Indian -2, yearnin' (free Mexico from invaders and set her on the road to greatness) -5
Gear: Winchester '73 rifle, double-action Colt Peacemaker, 50 rounds of ammunition for both guns, horse

TYPICAL JUARISTA

As you can see, *Juarista* rebels are not nearly as well trained as professional soldiers—but what they lack in skill they make up for in heart and tenacity.

PROFILE: TYPICAL JUARISTA

Corporeal: D:2d6, N:3d6, S:2d6, Q:2d6, V:4d6

Climbin' 1d6, dodge 1d6, fightin': brawlin' 1d6, horse ridin' 2d6, shootin': rifle 3d6

Mental: C:2d6, K:2d6, M:3d6, Sm:2d6, Sp:2d6

Spanish 2d6, search 2d6, survival: desert 3d6, trackin' 2d6
Pace: 8
Wind: 12
Gear: Rifle, 20 rounds of ammo, rations

A RATTLER IN THEIR MIDST

Bascomb doesn't know it, but the Juaristas have been hit hard by the Legion a couple of times recently. They've been tricked into going after targets which were secretly protected by companies of Legionnaires or Mexican soldiers. The real reason for this, which not even Juárez yet suspects, is that the Juaristas have a traitor in their ranks.

Itamar Tavarez Quivera y Higera was a low-level official in Juárez's government when the French invaded. Believing in Juárez's cause, he fled with his leader when Juárez left the capital. At first he fought loyally and well, gaining the rank of lieutenant.

However, with the passing years, he's become sick of living the bandit's life, and started to long for a return to the relatively luxurious life-style he used to have. Slowly he convinced himself that Juárez's cause was hopeless—and from there it didn't take him much to start passing information about the Juaristas to Santa Anna—who, of course, has promised Quivera the moon in exchange. If Juárez doesn't tumble to what's going on soon, Quivera could bring the Juarista crusade to a very abrupt halt very soon.

THE PHANTOM GENERAL

Everything the main text has to say about Díaz is true. He's a power hungry man who brooks no challenges to his authority. He's killed men before for questioning his orders, and he'll do it again. He doesn't care about causes or popularity. He wants control of Mexico, and he's more than willing to use fear, intimidation, and murder to get it. The Reckoners just love this guy.

The fearsome reputation Diaz has cultivated has a unique side effect. Whenever the locals know that he is operating in an area, the Fear Level immediately jumps by 1.

PROFILE: GENERAL PORFIRIO DIAZ MORY

Corporeal: D:4d10, N:2d12, S:3d6, Q:4d8, V:3d6

Dodge 2d12, fightin': brawlin', saber 3d12, horse ridin' 5d12, quick draw: pistol 3d8, shootin': pistol, rifle 4d10, sneak 3d12, swimmin' 2d12

Mental: C:3d8, K:3d6, M:4d10, Sm:3d6, Sp:2d6

Academia: military theory 4d6, academia: Mexican history and politics 3d6, area knowledge (Mexico) 6d6, artillery: cannons 3d8, guts 4d6, leadership 4d10, overawe 5d10, ridicule 3d6, Spanish 2d6, survival: desert, jungle, mountains 3d8, trackin' 3d8

Pace: 12
Wind: 12
Edges: Nerves o' steel 1, rank (general) 5, renown 5, sense of direction 1, social class: criollo 2, "the stare" 1, "the voice" (threatening) 1
Hindrances: Mean as a rattler -2, vengeful -3, yearnin' (conquer Mexico) -5
Gear: Rifle (varies), pistol (varies), saber, exceptional horse (fast)

THE PORFIRIATISTAS

Use the Mexican Soldier write-up for Díaz's men, but replace *fightin': lance* with *trackin'*—spears just get in the way when you're riding through the Yucatán jungle, but being able to hide your tracks comes in real handy.

One-Eyed Rafael

That bullet which took Rafael Velasco-Burgos's eye did more than that—it killed him. But not for long. Fortunately for him, it didn't tear up his thinker too much, and in a few days he came back Harrowed. According to the way he told it, he woke up after the battle and stumbled into a village where the *campesinos* nursed him back to health. The village was "destroyed by the French" shortly after he left (read: he killed everyone and burned the village to the ground so they couldn't tell anyone about him). Unfortunately for him, he didn't get them all and some of the survivors are looking for revenge.

Velasco-Burgos and his manitou get along just fine. He doesn't mind going along with the ideas it whispers in his mind from time to time. He plans to stick close to Díaz until the time is ripe, then kill him and take over his position as *el jefe*.

Profile: Velasco-Burgos

Corporeal: D:4d8, N:3d10, S:2d12, Q:3d8, V:4d8

Climbin' 2d10, dodge 2d10, fightin': brawlin', saber 3d10, shootin': pistol, rifle 5d8, sneak 2d10, swimmin' 2d10, throwin': balanced 3d8

Mental: C:2d8, K:2d6, M:4d8, Sm:1d6, Sp:2d8

Academia: military theory 1d6, artillery: cannons 1d8, gamblin' 2d6, guts 3d8, Spanish 2d6, overawe 5d8, scrutinize 2d8, search 2d8, survival: desert, jungle 3d6, tale-tellin' 4d6, trackin' 1d8

Pace: 10

Wind: 22

Edges: Brawny 3, the stare 1, social class: mestizo 1, tough as nails 3, "the voice" (threatening) 1

Hindrances: Bloodthirsty -2, enemy (survivors of the village massacre who are trying to track him down) -1, grim servant o' death -5, mean as a rattler -2, vengeful -3

Special Abilities:

    Harrowed: Dominion: Harrowed 4/ manitou 4, Powers: Berserker 4, eulogy 2

    Gear: Winchester '73 rifle, Colt Open Top revolver, 30 rounds of ammunition for both guns, knife, 50' rope.

Meet The Padre

Although there are more than a few corrupt or apologist priests out there, the average *padre* your posse runs across is likely to be just a plain, simple, devout man who believes deeply in God and wants nothing more than to help his flock through the travails of life. Priests wield considerable influence all over the country; your posse couldn't ask for a better ally than the local *sacerdote* (or a worse enemy).

Profile: Typical Village Priest

Corporeal: D:2d6, N:2d8, S:2d6, Q:2d4, V:3d6

Climbin' 1d8, dodge 1d8, horse ridin' 1d8, shootin': pistol 1d8, swimmin' 1d8

Mental: C:3d8, K:3d6, M:4d6, Sm:3d6, Sp:2d10

Faith 3d10, guts 3d10, Spanish 2d6, Latin 2d6, overawe 3d6, persuasion 3d6, professional: theology (Catholic) 3d6, tale-tellin' 3d6

Pace: 8

Wind: 16

Miracles: Protection

Edges: Fuero 3, renown (local priest) 1

Hindrances: Obligation (minister to his flock) -1, pacifist -5, self-righteous -3

Gear: Crucifix, Bible, prayer beads

Mexican Indians

Marshal, Pinnacle's fine book *Ghost Dancers* will tell you everything you need to know about the Apaches. *Ghost Dancers* doesn't cover the Maya, Zapotec, or other Mexican tribes, though.

Most Mexican Indians are *converted*—they no longer follow their ancestral ways enough to have guardian spirits or become shamans. Many are also *half-breeds*—or *mestizos*, as they say in Spanish. However, some pure-blooded, mostly uncivilized Indians (and that includes pretty much all the Apache) still live in Mexico. These Indians can

become shamans, though their shamanism often isn't much like what you'll find up north. Refer to the chapters on the Aztecs for some general ideas; most Meso-American Indian cultures borrowed heavily from each others' cultures.

The following guardian spirits are available to traditional Mexican Indians: Coyote, Crow, Eagle (but it functions like Raven), Owl, Snake, Spider, Turtle, Wolf. They can also take Jaguar (which has the same effect as Buffalo), Monkey (which has the same effect as Elk), or Hummingbird (or Quetzal) (either of which has the same effect as Eagle).

If your posse members are looking to play a member of the Aztecs, refer them to Chapter Three. It's entirely up to you, Marshal, if you wish to allow these characters in your game.

THE BORDER REGION

In general, the border region is Fear Level 3.

THE RIVER

The Rio Grande Region – Fear Level 3

There are more nasty things in and around the Rio Grande than the occasional cougar or jaguar. Those disappearing people and mangled bodies Bascomb mentioned aren't always just accidents.

DON'T DRINK THE WATER

Animals, cattle, and people all drink from the Rio Grande—it's a bountiful source of water in an otherwise arid country. But there's a type of creature living in the water, a relative of the tummy twister, that takes advantage of that fact to grow to maturity.

The Texas blood baby, as it's come to be known, only infects women. It has no use for men, and simply passes out of their bodies if drunk by them. Women aren't so lucky. Once a blood baby gets into a woman's stomach, it stays there and begins to grow. When it reaches the size of a finger or so, it claws its way out of the stomach and into the woman's womb. This causes a Light wound to the guts, which can't be negated with Fate Chips; it feels like, and is often mistaken for, a bad ulcer.

After it gets into the womb, the blood baby begins to grow quickly. Soon the woman's stomach begins to balloon up, just like she was pregnant—much to her embarrassment in many cases. But there's worse to come.

The growing blood baby will start to "kick," causing a permanent Heavy wound to the guts (again, no stopping the damage with Fate Chips). After about three to four weeks of "gestation," the blood baby's ready to be born. It rips its way out of the woman—causing a Critical guts wound (still no Fate Chips!) and almost certainly killing her—and attacks the nearest living thing it can, trying to consume as much of its flesh and blood as possible. Once it's eaten its weight in fresh meat, it makes for the nearest body of moving water to lay its "eggs" and start the whole cycle over again. Then it finds more victims to feed on.

Boiling Rio Grande water before its drunk kills any blood baby "fingerlings" in the water. Once one gets inside a woman, though, there isn't much which can be done to save her from at least some harm. Surgery, requiring a Hard (9) *medicine: surgery* roll, can get at the thing once it's in her womb, but it can fight back, with Traits proportionate to its age (a half-grown blood baby has Traits half as strong, for example).

PROFILE: TEXAS BLOOD BABY

Corporeal: D:3d6, N:3d6, S:2d8, Q:3d10, V:2d8
Dodge 5d6, fightin': brawlin' 5d6
Mental: C:2d6, K:1d6, M:1d6, Sm:1d6, Sp:1d4
Overawe 4d6
Pace: 6
Size: 2
Wind: 12
Terror: 9
Special Abilities:
  Bite: STR
  Claws: STR+1
Description: A grown blood baby looks like a perverted, twisted, malformed human baby with needle-sharp fangs, ragged claws on its hands and feet, blood-red skin covered with a matching mucous-like slime, and a slightly hunched back. It's a face not even a "mother" could love.

DON'T GO SWIMMIN', EITHER

Even if you don't drink from it, the Rio Grande's not all that safe. There's another abomination stalking its banks and waters—a sort of cross between a boa constrictor, a lamprey, and the Lernean hydra from Greek mythology. It's called a *serpiente sangrienta.*

An average serpiente sangrienta has 2-12 "tentacles," each up to six feet long and as thick around as a man's forearm. The end of each tentacle ends in a lamprey-like mouth which can latch onto a victim, bore through his flesh, and suck his blood. The tentacles all come together at one end to form a body at least three feet long. The thing's

heart and brain are located there; the body pulses with the beat of the heart. Much larger specimens exist, but they are rare.

Serpientes sangrientas prefer to go after large prey—people, cattle, or large animals, mostly—since they need plenty of flesh and blood to survive. After it's sucked a victim dry, it leaves the body to be torn at by vultures and other scavengers, making the death look like a wild animal attack.

PROFILE: SERPIENTE SANGRIENTA

Corporeal: D:3d8, N:3d10, S:3d10, Q:4d10, V:3d6
Fightin': brawlin' 4d10
Mental: C:2d6, K:1d6, M:2d6, Sm:1d6, Sp:1d4
Overawe 4d6
Pace: 10
Size: 7
Wind: 10
Terror: 11
Special Abilities:
  Bite: The serpiente sangrienta's bite initially does 1d6 damage. After making a bite, it latches on, and may do damage each round thereafter until removed without having to roll again to hit the victim or use an action. The creature continues to gnaw at the victim until it does a *heavy* wound to the affected area. Then it begins to suck blood, draining 1d4 points per round until the victim is dead. Pulling an attached tentacle off of a victim requires an Opposed *Strength* contest. If successful, the victim takes 1d4 damage and is free.
  Multiple Attacks: A serpiente sangrienta can make one attack with each tentacle per round, on the same or different victims, provided it obtains enough card (each tentacle attack counts as a single action).

Constriction: A tentacle can be used to hold a victim still instead of biting. An Opposed *Strength* contest is required to pry the tentacle loose.

Description: See text.

The Northern Desert

Most of the Sonora Desert and surrounding area is Fear Level 2, except near the lairs of certain abominations or other places noted below.

El Escorpión

For this feared bandito leader's men, you can use the *Bandito* Archetype in *Law Dogs*, Marshal. El Escorpión himself is a little better than that, though.

He has adopted the scorpion as his namesake due to an encounter he once had with a giant vinegaroon. He claims one of these beasts stung him and he was immune to its poison.

Profile: El Escorpión

Corporeal: D:4d12, N:3d12, S:3d6, Q:3d8, V:3d10

Dodge 2d12, fightin': brawlin', knife 3d12, gunplay 3d12, horse ridin' 3d12, quick draw: pistol 4d8, shootin': pistol, rifle 5d12, sneak 4d12, swimmin' 1d12, throwin': balanced 2d12

Mental: C:3d8, K:2d6, M:3d10, Sm:3d6, Sp:2d6

Area knowledge (northern Mexico) 3d6, gamblin' 4d6, guts 4d6, Spanish 2d6, overawe 3d10, ridicule 3d6, survival: desert 3d8, trackin' 3d8

Pace: 12

Wind: 20

Edges: Nerves o' steel 1, "the stare" 1, thick-skinned 3, tough as nails 2, "the voice" (threatening) 1

Hindrances: Bloodthirsty -2, outlaw -4, vengeful -3

Gear: Bullard Express rifle, Colt Frontier, 40 rounds of ammunition for both pistols, knife, rope, horse.

Canyons o' Blood

Copper Canyon—Fear Level 3

Copper Canyon is neither pleasant nor safe. People still live there since there's silver to be mined, but there are fewer of them every day.

Wall Crawlers

The cliff sides and peaks of the *barrancas* (canyons) are a perfect habitat for wall crawlers, and plenty of them have made their homes here. Any posses which have to go climbing or hiking in the area may very well run into one—or two, or three....

For another abominations which haunts the canyon, check out the Barranca Prowler on page 116.

Piedras Gemiras

Bascomb mentioned how the early Spanish settlers used Indian *esclavos* (slaves) to work their claims. In places, you could practically carpet the canyon floor with the bones of the Indians who died in the nearby silver mines. With the coming of the Reckoning, the immense amount of suffering which seeped into the rocks in these areas have been given a cruel form of life. This phenomena is known as *piedras gemiras* ("Moanin' Stones").

Piedras gemiras are sort of like emotional quicksand—anyone who gets too close runs the risk of being sucked into a maelstrom of long-forgotten human misery and torment. The spirits of the Indians who died here in such despair have been given voices, and those voices attract victims on which they temporarily slake their unquenchable anger. Their powers cannot affect other Indians, only white men.

Moanin' stones make a moaning sort of noise which sounds like a man in agony or turmoil. This is sure to attract anyone who doesn't know better. Once that person gets within ten feet of the rocks, he takes 2d6 Wind damage (or 3d6 if of Spanish descent) as an emotional backlash hits him full-force. As long as he remains within at least ten feet of them, he keeps taking 2d6 Wind per round until he pretty much

passes out. At that point, it's probably all over. Unless someone rescues him, or a barranca prowler or some other predator eats him (not likely, animals have learned to avoid areas of piedras gemiras), he'll die of starvation or dehydration there—every time he tries to wake up, the stones' moaning knocks him right back out, until his body and spirit eventually part ways.

If a potential victim has the good sense to plug his ears (with, say, cotton or wax) before approaching piedras gemiras, or he manages to stuff them shut before he falls unconscious, he takes only 1d6 Wind damage per round. Some enterprising banditos have learned to take advantage of this by plugging their ears, waiting near piedras gemiras for victims, and then robbing and killing the poor sods before they awake.

Characters can destroy piedras gemiras in two ways. First, they can simply destroy all the infested rock. That's likely to take dynamite, a mining crew, or something similar. Most of these rocks are about the size of a typical outhouse. Second, a good *exorcism* or similar miracle can send the tormented Indian souls on to the Happy Hunting Ground or whatever other reward they're entitled to.

The Taracha

Many years ago, the war chiefs of the Apache drove from their people a degenerate group of tribesmen who were discovered to be performing rituals in which children captured from other tribes were sacrificed and eaten. Supposedly, these Indians believed that such children represented the soul of their people, and that by sacrificing and eating them they could destroy that soul, and thus triumph over their enemies easily. While the Apaches fight hard and give no quarter to their foes, they considered such practices abhorrent and cast the offenders out.

These fallen Apache fled into the Copper Canyon region, where they soon encountered the Tarahumara. Most Tarahumara were as disgusted by them as their Apache brethren, but they swayed a few bands to their side. Eventually these groups interbred, creating a tribe called the Taracha.

Today the Taracha, a deeply inbred and malevolent group of Indians, still stalk the canyons, kidnapping and eating children. The Tarahumara and local residents fear them so much they won't even speak the tribe's name. Their shamans, including their powerful chief Heart Like Fire, have powers more like black magic than standard shaman rituals and favors, and use childrens' blood to create cave paintings and as war paint.

Another important Taracha ritual centers around the drinking of *tesguino*, a fermented corn beverage. Taracha warriors consume it before going into battle, and the effects of the "corn beer," combined with the frenzy of the ritual, gives them an increase of +1 die type on their *Strength* and *Vigor* for about an hour.

The Taracha have begun to seek women with which to enlarge their tribe. They kidnap non-Taracha women, rape them, and then kill them after they give birth to a new Taracha baby.

Monterrey

Fear Level 2

Despite the presence of a large cathedral and a Catholic bishop, there's something unholy about Monterrey. Many residents seem to scurry around furtively, afraid of drawing attention to themselves. Others, including the Legionnaires and those who cavort with them, seem intent on eating, drinking, and being merry, as if they can stave off the lurking darkness with *joie de vivre*.

Observant characters note, after spending a little time in the city, that there don't seem to be very many children around anywhere. Most Mexican towns have a lot of children playing in the streets, but Monterrey has none—the few they see are always accompanied by parents who hurry them away before any "strangers" can get a close look at them. The residents of the town are unwilling to talk to outsiders about the situation in Monterrey.

The Obispado Curse

When the Legion kicked the Bishop out of his house so they could use it as a military headquarters, it called down a terrible sort of curse upon the city, courtesy of the Reckoners. Ever since then, all children born in the city have been malformed and sickly. They often don't even live beyond their sixth birthday; those who do have become ugly in both body and soul.

Some of these *obispiños* have unleashed their latent rage and evil on the local dogs and cats (a few of whom may have returned as undead critters to stalk their tormentors); others have taken to attacking people. Strangers make the perfect targets, since few

Monterreyans care what happens to them. Your posse may soon find itself surrounded by a pack of dirty, fiendish children wielding rusty knives, cleavers, hooks, and similar makeshift weapons.

The only way to lift the Obispado curse is to get the Legion to apologize to the bishop sincerely and ask his forgiveness, give him back his residence, and leave Monterrey altogether. Good luck.

Profile: Obispinos

Corporeal: D:2d6, N:1d8, S:1d6, Q:2d6, V:2d6

Climbin' 1d6, fightin': brawlin', knife 2d8, sneak 4d8

Mental: C:2d6, K:1d4, M:2d4, Sm:1d6, Sp:1d4

Overawe 4d4

Pace: 8

Size: 3-4

Wind: 10

Terror: 7

Special Abilities:

Weapons: The childrens' weapons typically do STR+1d6. Because they're rusty, they may cause an injured character to develop lockjaw. A wounded hero must make an Onerous (7) *Vigor* roll to avoid the infection. Failure means a case of lockjaw. Treat this as the *ailin': fatal* Hindrance or use the rules found in *Deadlands Dispatch #4* in *Back East South.*

Bite: The children can bite for STR+1d4 points of damage.

Description: A wickedly malformed, dirty little child with a look of pure evil about it.

Sometimes the Worm Eats You

For some reason, bottles of tequila usually have a worm in the bottom of 'em. Don't ask us why, they just do. Some tequila distillers have found that a small tentacle from a Mojave rattler works even better!

Somehow, putting one of these tentacles in with the tequila makes it stronger and more intoxicating than ever. But watch out—sometimes that "worm's" not all the way dead! An unwary cowboy who doesn't keep his eye on it when he drinks may find it lashing out to slide down his throat and into his stomach. Then all the tequila in Mexico won't dull the pain as the thing rips him apart from inside.

PROFILE: MOJAVE WORM

Corporeal: D:1d6, N:2d8, S:2d6, Q:2d8, V:2d6
Fightin': brawlin' 2d8
Mental: C:1d4, K:1d4, M:2d4, Sm:1d4, Sp:1d4
Pace: 1
Size: 1
Wind: 5
Terror: 5
Special Abilities:
  Rippin': A Mojave worm has hard, horny ridges along part of its length which can tear through flesh pretty easily. They do STR+1d4 damage normally, and STR+2d6 when the worm gets to attack some unlucky bastard from inside his own stomach.
Description: A greyish-brown thing like a large worm.

A LEGION OF TROUBLES

While the Legionnaires in Monterrey generally enjoy "the good life" a lot more than their comrades posted to other garrisons in Mexico, that doesn't mean they take it easy on troublemakers. Any posse members who come to Monterrey and start trouble, or even look like it, attract the unwanted attention of dozens, or even hundreds, of testy Legionnaires.

Although they don't know why many of them feel vaguely guilty for the goings-on in the town. This is a new experience for many of the Legions cutthroats and it makes them edgy. They deal with this by beating the snot out of anyone who crosses them—which is anybody who doesn't immediately kowtow to them.

SANTA ISABELLA

Fear Level 4
Bascomb's absolutely right in his assessment of the town of Santa Isabella. An abomination called a Massacre Spirit, composed of the

collective enraged souls of the slaughtered Legionnaires, attacks any Mexicans it can catch alone and any strangers who come to town (so you're posse's in for a big surprise if they hear about strange events and come to investigate).

PROFILE: MASSACRE SPIRIT

Corporeal: D:3d10, N:3d10, S:3d8, Q:4d12, V:3d8
Dodge 3d10, fightin': brawlin', saber 4d10, quick draw: rifle 4d8, shootin': rifle 4d10, sneak 5d10
Mental: C:3d6, K:2d6, M:3d8, Sm:2d6, Sp:3d8
Overawe 6d8
Pace: 15
Size: 8
Wind: 20

Terror: 9

Special Abilities:

Battle Terror: The Massacre Spirit can inspire in its foes the terror of being ambushed and slaughtered. As a single action it can engage in an opposed *Spirit* roll against a victim. If it wins, the victim loses 2 levels from his *dodge, fightin', shootin',* and other combat-related Aptitudes because he becomes panicked with the fear of his own death. This effect lasts for 1d6+1 rounds, and may only be used once on any given character in any given fight with the Massacre Spirit.

Undead.

Weapons: The Massacre Spirit carries a chassepot and a saber. These weapons work normally against most opponents, but against Mexicans they inflict double damage.

Description: The Massacre Spirit looks like a huge, bloody, bullet-riddled soldier dressed in the scraps of a Legionnaire's uniform. His eyes seem to glow with a supernatural anger and his features are twisted into a mask of rage.

CENTRAL MEXICO

Because it's more settled and "civilized," most parts of this region are Fear Level 2

MEXICO CITY

Fear Level 3

MONTEZUMA'S REVENGE

Something Bascomb doesn't mention, because it hasn't yet affected him, is how many people—especially strangers—get sick from drinking the water in Mexico City. This isn't a fluke; it's the result of a curse laid on the waters of the Valley of Mexico by Montezuma himself. Before Cortés killed him, he realized that the time of the Aztecs had passed—or so he thought—and that the Spaniards would build their own city in the place of Tenochtitlan. As a form of revenge, he laid a curse on the Valley's precious waters, that they would make the Spaniards sick when drunk.

That curse was just so much hot air until the Reckoning happened. In 1863, Pestilence kicked it into high gear. Now, any person without at least half Indian blood can get sick mighty easily if they drink the water. For every day such a person drinks Mexico City water, he must make an Onerous (7) *Vigor* roll or succumb to a stomach-twisting malady which reduces his *Strength* and *Vigor* die types by 2 (minimum of d4) and makes him run for the outhouse a lot. These effects last for 1d4 days. If the character restricts his liquids to things other than water, or always boils his water before he drinks it, he will not contract the illness. Once the hero has overcome this illness, he develops an immunity to it.

BUILDINGS O' BLOOD

The *tezontle* stone in Cortés-era buildings sometimes does more than resemble dried blood—it actually oozes real blood! This doesn't happen often, and the blood doesn't gush out—it's a subtle effect that only one or two characters are likely to notice. Anyone noticing this has to make an Onerous (7) *guts* check or suffer a 4d6 roll on the Scart Table. Any phobia developed because of the roll is hematophobia, the fear of blood.

CATHEDRAL O' GOLD

A holy place sanctified by generations of worshippers and saintly men, the Cathedral of Mexico offers refuge to the fearful multitudes who have fallen afoul of the Reckoners' influences. It cancels the effects of the area's Fear Level for anyone inside it. In fact, all *guts* rolls made while within its walls receive a +1 bonus to the roll. Furthermore, you should reduce the Target Numbers for all blessed miracles used within the Cathedral by 2.

IT'S ALL HAPPENING AT THE ZOO

The *Jardín Zoológica* gives you a chance to throw all sorts of strangeness at your posse, Marshal. Some of it may actually be Reckoner-created horror, such as a jaguar which turns out to be a nagual, or an ordinary animal warped by the energies of the Reckoning.

However, even some completely natural animals may astound and terrify the posse. For example, few folks from 1877 America had ever seen a gorilla, even in a picture book. Imagine what they'd think about one which broke free from the zoo and started rampaging through the streets of Mexico City. Sure looks like an abomination, don't it?

TEOTIHUACÁN

Teotihuacán is one of the most important sacred sites of the Secret Empire, and as such they guard it fiercely. Characters approaching it may be waylaid by Jaguar and Eagle warriors and Aztec sorcerers. The Aztecs tolerate the presence of the white scientists who excavate the site, since they are uncovering more and more of the sacred buildings. However, when Xitlan judges that enough digging has been done, the archaeologists will be seized and sacrificed. Until then, the professors get to do the Aztecs' work for them.

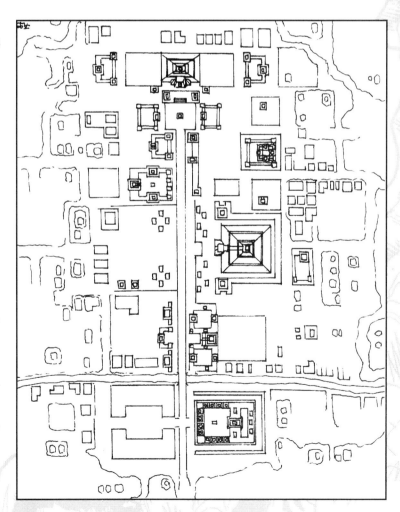

THE STARS ARE RIGHT

One of the reasons Teotihuacán holds such importance is that any Aztec blood magic ceremonies performed there on the appropriate pyramid on days or nights when the sun or stars align with that pyramid are particularly powerful. Increase the priest's levels in all of his black magic powers by +2 (see page 108 for details on particular Aztec black magic). It's possible for a power to exceed level 5 under these conditions. The exact effect of this is up to you, Marshal.

THE SCREAMING FIELDS

The Aztecs guard the fields near Teotihuacán just as heavily as the ruins themselves (albeit with disguised warriors), since that's where the Lords of the Obsidian Blade grow *plantagrito*, the Reckoning-spawned plant which allows them to control Santa Anna's Army of the Dead. They harvest the plants at night (since their screams might attract too much attention during the day), and only when the archaeologists have left for a while or been lured away. They take the harvested plants to Mexico City, where servants of the Lords process them into the zombie drug.

POTS AND BONES

Artifacts found at Teotihuacán, such as the bones of inhabitants or the items they crafted, may be powerful relics (whether for good or evil). Such things should provide you with plenty of story ideas, Marshal. For example, suppose a posse member managed to find a powerful Aztec relic, and then had to deal with the servants of the Secret Empire sent after him to "retrieve" it?

In addition, some of the archeologists have become suspicious of some of the strange goings-on at the site. Professor Riley is looking to hire on some guards at the rate of $1 day.

GUADALAJARA

Fear Level 2

CANYON CRAWLERS

The Oblatos Canyon is a deep, dark place where most Tapatíos don't like to go—only the rough, tough miners and folks too desperately poor to fear it descend into its depths.

Why, you ask? Simple—plenty of wall crawlers and barranca prowlers roam around here. In fact, they're common enough that local folks accept their existence, the way that people in the Great Maze accept California Maze dragons. There's a bounty of 2,500 pesos for every crawler or prowler head brought to Mayor Delpaiz's office. So far, the denizens of the canyon are winning the head count.

THE WHITE ALTAR

Bascomb's estimate of the marble altar's age is off by a year; it's 14 years old. In short, it was carved in 1863—right after the Reckoning occurred. The artist was an eccentric fellow named Paolo Tarrucelli, who became *really* deranged after a manitou took up residence inside his already warped brain.

Thus, the supposedly religious carvings on the altar actually contain many cleverly disguised blasphemous and occult symbols which spoil the effects of the altar and the church, preventing it from having the same effects as the Basilica (see below). Any blessed who touches the altar feels a "wrongness" about it, but nothing more. Only a character with *academia: occult* at level 4 or higher who makes a Hard (9) *scrutinize* roll can figure out what's wrong with the altar.

LA ZAPOPONISTA

La Zapoponista is, in fact, a holy relic. Not only does it sometimes cure peoples' afflictions (such as blindness or lameness), it sanctifies the entire Basilica. Inside the building the effects of the area's Fear Level 2 are cancelled, and the Target Numbers for all blessed miracles used within the Cathedral are reduced by 2.

MARSHAL

There are no hard and fast rules for La Zapoponista's miracles, Marshal—it's a plot device. Use it if doing so would help your story; otherwise don't worry about it. However, it makes a good scenario seed—evil folks wanting to get their hands on it might try to steal it during its five-month tour of Jalisco, for example, meaning that the posse has to get it back for the Basilica.

THE LAKE MONSTER

Not too long ago, one of Cipactli's Children (see page 118) took up residence in Lake Chapala. The people who disappeared became its meals. However, they haven't done much to sate its hunger. Soon it will be forced to eat more people, or even to slither on down to Guadalajara and snap up a few unsuspecting Tapatíos—which is sure to send the area's Fear Level skyrocketing.

VERACRUZ

Fear Level 2

LOST TREASURES OF VERACRUZ

With all the gold and silver that left Mexico through this port, and all the pirate attacks, inevitably some of that treasure got lost in the shuffle. Several places throughout town, or in the waters of the port itself, contain caches of gold, silver, and even loot from the Aztec Empire. Having your posse stumble across one of these is a good way to give them a stake to fund some adventure, or perhaps inflict a cursed relic upon them. The hunt for long-lost gold could even become an adventure in and of itself.

SAN JUAN DE ULÚA

The Reckoning's passed the infamous Veracruz prison by—so far. The evil out there is of the purely human variety: jailers torturing inmates, prisoners killing each other for scraps of food, and other brutality. Posse members who get tossed in there are in for an unpleasant time. Bascomb wasn't exaggerating when he mentioned how hard it is to escape from the prison.

CARNAVAL OF TERROR

The reason so many people have been dying or disappearing during Carnaval isn't Los Hermanos—it's something far more sinister. Never ones who could resist turning a good time bad, the Reckoners have let loose a fiendish abomination called *El Bufón* ("The Clown").

Able to appear as either a handsome man or a gorgeous woman, El Bufón always wears the happiest and most exotic Carnaval garb. With his good looks and charming, sexy personality, he lures unsuspecting partygoers away from the main crowds, then tortures them and drinks their blood until they die. His appearance changes each time, so witnesses' descriptions are useless.

Profiles: El Bufón

Corporeal: D:2d8, N:3d8, S:3d12+2, Q:5d12, V:4d10
Dodge 2d8, fightin': brawlin' 4d8, sneak 8d8
Mental: C:2d8, K:2d6, M:3d6, Sm:3d6, Sp:3d6
Overawe 4d6, scrutinize 3d8, search 3d8
Pace: 10
Size: 6
Wind: NA
Terror: 7
Special Abilities:

Claws: El Bufón can cause its hands to grow into wicked claws which do STR+1d4 damage.

Feast Of Blood: If El Bufón gets a raise on a *fightin': brawlin'* roll, it latches onto a victim's neck with its mouth and begins sucking blood. This does 1d6 Wind damage each round. The only way to stop it is to win an opposed *Strength* roll contest. While sucking blood, El Bufón can also use its claws on the victim, though it rarely does so because it can't drink blood he spills. For every full 6 points of Wind damage the creature inflicts in this manner, its *Strength* die increases by a step. This effect lasts for 24 hours. If the posse catches up with El Bufón shortly after it feeds, they could be in trouble

Undead.

Description: See text. If El Bufón has a true form, no one has ever seen it.

Los Hermanos

For most members of Los Hermanos, use the Bandito or Desperado archetypes from *Law Dogs*, with minor changes as appropriate to represent specific members. For Efraín Alejo-Esparza, use the Bandito archetype, but increase all of his Corporeal Trait Aptitudes by 2, increase *fightin': knife* to 6 and his *overawe* to 5, give him *throwin': knife* 6d12, and replace the *oath* with *mean as a rattler* and *bloodthirsty*.

Camarón

Fear Level 4

The village of Camarón, where a company of the Legion was destroyed, remains abandoned even today—and with good reason. The remains of the dead Legionnaires still stalk the area, hoping to get revenge on the Mexicans who killed them and stole the gold they were guarding.

About half the Legionnaires are more or less intact, and are walkin' dead, though they cannot tolerate sunlight and only come out on overcast days or at night. Use the veteran legionnaire stats from page 76, but treat them as undead. Each has a *yearnin'* to recover the gold they lost and to kill Mexican soldiers—or even Mexican civilians, if they get the chance. They don't have very many working guns, though. The few they do have were taken from their victims; they're more likely to use knives, claws, or similar weapons.

However, there were quite a few Legionnaires who got so badly shot up that their bodies literally fell to pieces. These pieces have also become from beyond, and crawl, walk, or slither around the abandoned village.

For most body parts, this is just revolting. Arms and heads are another matter, though. Arms can attack with *fightin': brawlin'* 3d8 and a *Strength* of 3d6. Heads only have *fightin': brawlin'* 1d6, and if successful bite for 1d6 points of damage. These severed body parts have a size of 3 and are destroyed as soon as they suffer a Maiming wound. If a Harrowed character destroys at least six of these dangerous corpse bits, as coup he gains the power *dead man's hand* at level 1.

Danjou's Hand

Also of note in Camarón is Danjou's hand. Captain Danjou, who led the doomed company, had lost his left hand some time before the battle, and it had been replaced with a carved wooden hand. That hand was lost during the battle, and it's now a relic.

Power: If attached to an arm without a hand, it bonds with that person's flesh and begins functioning as a normal, albeit wooden, hand. The hand has 3d12

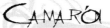

Strength or its owner's *Strength*, whichever is better, and it is considered to have 2 levels of Armor against all forms of damage except fire.

Taint: The "wearer" becomes *intolerant* of Mexicans.

SOUTHERN MEXICO

Most parts of southern Mexico are at least Fear Level 2, and many are level 3 or higher.

SACRED WELLS

The *cenotes*, or Mayan sacred wells, may appeal to posse members as a source of treasure. It's true that many precious objects were thrown into them, and characters willing to devote the time and effort can pull gold, jade, and valuable artifacts out of them. But there's more than gold in them thar wells. A few abominations have found them to be excellent homes as well. Some of them include:

CHAC, THE RAIN GOD

The principal reason for sacrificing women (or sometimes children or men) by throwing them in cenotes was to exhort the Rain God, Chac, who was said to live below the greenish-black waters of the cenote, to send rain. But

what they were really doing was *placating* Chac—an alligator-like type of abomination which lives in many of the larger, darker cenotes and gobbles up sacrifices whenever it can get them. These days, when sacrifices generally aren't available, unwary peasants, explorers, archaeologists, and posse members do just fine. Really hungry creatures sometimes climb out of their wells and do some sight-seeing.

PROFILES: CHAC

Corporeal: D:2d6, N:2d6, S:5d12+8, Q:2d8, V:5d12
Dodge 1d6, fightin': brawlin' 4d6, sneak 5d6, swimmin' 8d6
Mental: C:2d6, K:1d4, M:4d8, Sm:2d6, Sp:1d4
Overawe 6d8
Pace: 4 running/10 swimming
Size: 9
Wind: 40
Terror: 9
Special Abilities:
  Armor: Chac's leathery skin provides him with 2 levels of armor.
  Bite: STR+2d12
  Claws: STR+2d6

Description: Chacs look like goggle-eyed alligator-men with clawed arms and legs (which are also webbed for fast swimming), tails, faces like a cross between an alligator and a child, and leather-like skin which is mostly green and black, but has patches of dull red.

Tears O' Blood

Not all the women who were sacrificed to the gods went to their fate willingly. Some fought against it, and hated and despised those who killed them. Some of these women have now become abominations which live near the cenotes and prey on those who come to them. They're known as *balac kchab*—"blood-weeping woman"—because those who have survived an encounter with them say that they cry tears of blood.

Profiles: Balac Kchab

Corporeal: D:2d8, N:1d10, S:2d6, Q:3d6, V:3d6
Dodge 2d10, fightin': brawlin' 3d10, sneak 6d10, swimmin' 3d10

Mental: C:4d8, K:1d6, M:3d8, Sm:2d6, Sp:1d6
Overawe 4d8, scrutinize 2d8, search 2d8
Pace: 10
Size: 6
Wind: 12
Terror: 9
Special Abilities:
  Bloody Tears: Anyone who touches a balac kchab's bloody tears (which may occur during a Watery Kiss) may be overwhelmed by the terror and rage which these creatures feel. Roll a contest of *Spirit.* If the victim loses, he suffers a 4d6 roll on the Scart Table.
  Watery Kiss: With a successful *fightin': brawlin'* roll, a balak kchab can grab a victim and kiss him, spewing foul cenote waters into the victim's mouth, stomach, and lungs. This causes 2d6 damage to the guts (armor of any sort typically offers no protection). Furthermore, the victim loses all Action cards in his hand (including cards up his sleeve) because he falls to the ground gagging and spitting up water.
  Undead.
Description: Balack Kchab look something like the bloated corpses of drowned women, though a certain sorrowful beauty can be seen amid the horrid ugliness (which just makes that ugliness all the more terrifying). They constantly weep tears of blood.

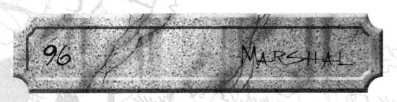

Marshal

THE SECRET EMPIRE

You've seen references to it earlier on in this book, Marshal. Now it's time for you to learn everything there is to know about the Secret Empire of the Aztecs!

AN UNDYING SORCERER

The story begins about 350 years ago with an old Aztec priest named Three Death. Way back in the early 1500s, among the many priests who served the gods in Tenochtitlan was Three Death. Although not the chief priest, or even close to that position, he stood out for his fanatical devotion to his duties, and the relish with which he performed them—especially the sacrifices. Thanks to his piety, the god Tezcatlipoca revealed to him some of the secrets of sorcery, which he began practicing in secret.

Then came the day when word reached the Aztec court that Topiltzin Quetzalcoatl had returned! Three Death scoffed at these stories. As a devotee of Tezcatlipoca, he knew that the Plumed Serpent had been banished forever by the god of sorcery. Quetzalcoatl was powerless and would never return to Anahuac. Three Death realized that this was not an Aztec god who had arrived on the shores of the empire, but an invader.

As reports came in of the Spaniards' progression westward, Three Death, along with a few other lesser priests, urged Montezuma to action. He said that the "gods" were just strange-looking men, and that they must be destroyed. But Montezuma vacillated; he wanted to believe that Cortés was a god, and he would not throw away his hopes so easily. As the Spaniards got nearer and nearer to Tenochtitlan, Three Death gnashed his teeth in frustration. He was Cassandra to the Aztecs' Trojans.

Then the white-skinned men arrived. They were greeted with honor and dignity, but they repaid their Aztec hosts

with greed and destruction. Three Death had the satisfaction of seeing himself proved right, but it was a cold satisfaction indeed. His people seem to have laid down for the Spaniards like dogs.

Determined to provoke his people into casting the invaders out of the city—or, better yet, capturing and sacrificing them—Three Death worked a powerful magic of fear on the Spaniards to bring matters to a head. During the feast of Huitzilopochtli, it worked; the Spaniards, unreasonably terrified of what was just a dance and celebration because of Three Death's spell, slaughtered dozens of nobles and then took shelter in Montezuma's palace.

At last, the Aztecs realized the true nature of the Spaniards! Three Death became a leader of the forces who rejected everything the white men said and brought. He was in the forefront of the battle when Cortés returned, and killed more than a dozen Spaniards himself without suffering a single wound.

But his luck could not last. As the Spaniards fled the city on La Noche Triste, one of them turned and fired a last shot at the natives. It hit Three Death right in the heart, killing him. His body tumbled off the causeway into the bloody froth of Lake Texcoco.

THE RISE OF XITLAN

Before long, it washed up on the shores of the lake. But no vulture would touch it. Mictlantecuhtli, god of death, held the renegade priest in high esteem, and determined to breathe life back into him, that he might save his people from the Spanish yoke. Twenty days after falling to a Spanish bullet, Three Death arose and walked again. It was not truly life—no heart beat within his chest, and his lungs did not fill with air—but it was not death, and he was pleased at the gift the god had given him. To commemorate his new life, he decided to take on a new name. He called

SEEDS OF EMPIRE

Slowly, he and his followers spread the word to those Aztecs within whom the fires of devotion and empire still burned. Gradually they slipped away from their captors to join Xitlan in the wild places, where they could hide themselves from Spanish eyes and live their traditional life. Unwilling to sacrifice any of his small band of followers, Xitlan used captured Spaniards or traitorous Aztecs to feed the gods.

Xitlan and his followers soon realized that they would not overthrow the Spanish regime soon. The Spaniards were too powerful, and most of their people were too easily cowed. It would take years of effort and struggle to build up both their magical powers and the strength of their forces to the point where the Europeans could be challenged.

Xitlan knew he could afford to wait— he would never die. But his followers would. To maintain a self-sustaining priesthood through which religious and magical knowledge could be passed, he created the *Iztlecuhtle*, the Lords of the Obsidian Blade, a sort of "ruling council" for his people. He, of course, was the unquestioned leader of the Lords, and always would be.

THE SECRET EMPIRE

Seven New Fire ceremonies passed, and seven times Xitlan rekindled the fires, hoping that this time they brought the doom of the Spaniards. Every time his hopes were dashed. However, he never lost faith, and neither did the Lords of the Obsidian Blade and their followers. For generation after generation, they raised their children to follow traditional Aztec ways. Some of their followers were sent down to the white man's cities and *haciendas* to spy on them and learn their ways, the better that they might be defeated. Xitlan would not make the same mistake Montezuma did, that of underestimating the Spaniards.

Xitlan's followers soon infiltrated every level of Mexican society as servants. His power now encompassed not only the thousands of pure-blooded

himself *Xitlan,* from the Nahuatl word for "vengeance," for he intended to revenge himself on every white man who dared set foot in the lands of the Aztecs.

Xitlan wandered the wastes for a year, communing with Tezcatlipoca and the other gods and learning more sorcery. When he felt ready, he returned to Tenochtitlan, now called Mexico City, disguised as a humble porter. There he found that his fellow priests had been put into schools run by Franciscan monks to teach them Catholicism and Spanish. One by one he contacted them and revealed himself to them. Those who agreed to support his mission—and there were many—he let live. Those who turned their backs on the Aztec ways he killed, not even deigning to sacrifice their unworthy blood.

Aztecs who lived in hidden valleys and desert regions throughout Mexico, but a large group of well-placed spies. Perhaps in a fit of whimsy, he named his "nation" *Quetl Tloque Nahua,* the "Secret Empire of the Aztecs." His people refer to him as the Green Feather Emperor—a decidedly gentle and artistic-sounding title for one so versed in the arts of black magic, sorcery, violence, and death.

Storms And Ravens

Then, in the year 4 House, something truly amazing and wonderful happened. Xitlan suddenly found that his powers had increased a hundredfold, and that he could commune with the gods more clearly than he ever had. The Lords' powers also increased, though not so much as Xitlan's.

A year or two later, a mysterious Indian shaman from the north, calling himself Raven, found Xitlan. Somehow this inscrutable figure came straight to the Aztec sorcerer's very lair, bypassing guards and guardian spells as if they were nothing. But he did not come to harm Xitlan. He came to explain, and to seek alliance.

Raven revealed the truth behind the Reckoning to Xitlan, and explained to him what his powers were now capable of accomplishing. Xitlan agreed with Raven's goals—the destruction of the white men—and gladly pacted with him. Although rarely in contact with each other, as brothers they now strive to realize a common dream.

The Coming Of The Sixth Sun?

After his meeting with Raven, Xitlan realized that he might be able to bring his plans to fruition much more quickly. However, he knew that after years of isolation, he needed to gauge the strength of the enemy himself, and put himself in a position from which he could undermine the Mexican (and now French) forces. His spells soon revealed to him the man most susceptible to his influences: General Santa Anna.

Xitlan went to Santa Anna and, using his powers, convinced the general that he (Xitlan) was a shaman descended from the ancient Aztecs—a shaman who could use his powers to aid the general's schemes. Santa Anna listened, and believed—especially after Xitlan turned a corpse into a walking, fighting soldier before his very eyes! With such power at his beck and call, Santa Anna believes he will soon be unstoppable—and he could be right.

Xitlan and his minions are now poised in positions of power throughout the Empire of Mexico, ready to strike at the undead sorcerer's command. The year prophesied for the ending of the Fifth World is fast approaching, and Xitlan believes that he can usher in the Sixth Sun as he destroys the Spaniards, thereby perhaps becoming a god himself!

Some of his followers, including a few of the Lords, are not so sure, and they remain wary of Xitlan's grand scheme, but in their desire to retake Mexico for themselves, they are willing to overlook his planned apotheosis.

Xitlan

The leader of the Secret Empire, and the driving force behind it from the very beginning, is the Aztec sorcerer-priest Xitlan. Many who know of him, including Raven, think that he's simply a priest who came back from the dead Harrowed. While he does superficially resemble a Harrowed (and, for that matter, a walkin' dead) in some ways, he's not. He's been up and around and moving since long before Raven was born or the Reckoning conceived of, courtesy of the Aztec god of the dead. He doesn't have to fight any manitou for control of his body and mind. He's *undead*, not Harrowed.

Furthermore, that state, combined with his powers, makes him a master of lesser types of undead, including Harrowed and walkin' dead. He can create them, control them, or destroy them as he wishes. He's what the Germans would call a *liche*.

Xitlan possesses untrammelled ambition and greed for power. First, he wants to destroy all Mexicans (he still calls them "Spaniards") except for Aztecs and other native peoples. Where he used to have a heart, all he has now is a 350-year-old knot of bitterness, spite, and evil, all directed at those who took his people's homeland and enslaved them. Then, when he's accomplished that goal, he wants to take his place among the Aztec gods! He believes that if he offers them enough blood and hearts (say, from all those Spaniards he wants to get rid of), they'll admit him bodily to their ranks.

For now, Xitlan serves as a humble shaman advising General Santa Anna. Toadying to a Spaniard has only honed his hatred of them, but he believes that Santa Anna is one of the keys to his victory. He plans to lead Santa Anna back to the throne of Mexico, then, when he's at his most unsuspecting, unleash the forces of the Secret Empire to retake their land.

Note: the version of Xitlan below revises and replaces the one from *The Marshal's Handbook*.

PROFILE: XITLAN

Corporeal: D:3d8, N:3d8, S:4d10, Q:4d6, V:3d10
Climbin' 1d8, dodge 2d8, fightin': macahuitl 3d8, sneak 5d8, throwin': balanced, Aztec magic, bolts o' doom, spear 7d8
Mental: C:4d10, K:3d12, M:4d10, Sm:4d8, Sp:4d12
Academia: occult, Aztec culture and lore 10d12, bluff 4d8, faith 8d8, guts 7d8, Nahuatl 4d12, Spanish 2d12, English 1d12, French 1d12, leadership 6d10, medicine: general 5d12, overawe 7d10, scrutinize 5d10, search 4d10, survival: desert, mountains 5d8, trackin' 3d8
Pace: 8
Size: 6
Wind: 22

Edges: Arcane background: Aztec 3, good birth omens 5
Hindrances: Enemy (Priests of Quetzalcoatl) -5, intolerance ("Spaniards") -3, self-righteous -3, superstitious -2, vengeful -3, yearnin' (retake Mexico for Aztecs, become a god) -5
Special Abilities:
Black Magic: Animal mastery 4, bolts o' doom 4 (trappings: Xitlan projects a "smoking sun," or comet, at the target), cloak o' evil 3 (trappings: a protective jaguar skin covers Xitlan), create nagual, darts of mixcoatl, forewarning 4 (trappings: obsidian mirror), involuntary sacrifice 4, jaguar's swiftness 3, nahual 4, obsidian winds 5, pact 5, puppet 5, scrye 5 (trappings: obsidian mirror), skin of the pimply one 3, spook 3 (trappings: victim experiences a brief vision of himself being sacrificed), sun of the jaguar, zombie 5 (see below)
Mastery Of The Undead: Xitlan can create, control, and destroy undead. He creates them with his *zombie* spell, but he can use that spell to create other types of undead than walkin' dead—he can make a corpse come back Harrowed or as a zombie or nosferatu (see *Night Train*), for example. He can exert absolute control and dominance over a number of undead equal to his *Spirit* die type (*i.e.*, eight); others he must control through spells, persuasion, or force (that's why the Ejército de los Muertos will rampage if not fed plantagrito or brains. There are too many of them for him to control directly). Harrowed heroes may roll a contest of *Spirit* to resist this power, but Xitlan gets a +6 bonus to his roll. As a Speed 1 action, he can inflict 5d10 damage to any undead creature's noggin using his *throwin': bolts o' doom* Aptitude. This has a Range Increment of 10.
Ritual 8: fast, maim, paint, human sacrifice
Undead.
Description: Xitlan has the skin tone and typical facial features of a pure-blooded Aztec of early middle age,

but they seem somehow faded, suggesting that he may be older than he seems. Indeed, his entire body appears somewhat withered and desiccated, though not to the point where it would tip anyone off that he's not entirely alive. However, anyone who watches him closely for a few minutes may notice that he doesn't seem to breathe. He usually wears the simple garb of a lowly Aztec priest.

The Lords Of The Obsidian Blade

Xitlan's chief servants, and the rulers of the various hidden communities of the Secret Empire which are scattered across Mexico, are the Lords of the Obsidian Blade. Each of them is a powerful Aztec sorcerer-priest, like Xitlan himself, though they are nothing compared to him. While some of the Lords privately question his expressed goal of ascending into the Aztec heavens to join the gods, all of them support his goal of returning Mexico to Aztec rule, and they will work with him at least that long.

Some of the most prominent Lords include the following:

Four Jaguar

The most physically powerful of the Lords is a huge bear of a man named Four Jaguar. Ruler of an Aztec community located in a valley in western Mexico, Four Jaguar is a chief and son of chiefs. Since his earliest days his family has filled his head with tales of the brave deeds of his ancestors and the cruelty of the Spaniards who slaughtered them. He has been raised to hate white men with a passion, and he always looks forward to the next opportunity to kill a few of them. He yearns for the day when he can meet the Spaniards in open battle and split their bodies in two with his enormous two-handed macahuitl.

Except for this seething hatred, Four Jaguar is a gentle man and a good ruler with a gift for farming and leadership. His people admire and respect him greatly, and they don't hesitate to carry out his orders. He is one of the Lords who questions Xitlan's desire to attain godhood—but, of course he, only does so privately. Assuming someone could convince him that his lifelong hatred of

the Spaniards is wrong, he might even be persuaded to "switch sides."

Four Jaguar has over a dozen sons, one of whom, Ten Monkey, will succeed him as chief when the time comes. Although not likely to grow nearly as tall or strong as his father, Ten Monkey seems to make up in cleverness and guile what he lacks in strength. His people say that Huehuecoyotl has touched his heart. He looks to be a fine leader in his own right.

Four Jaguar is the war leader of the Secret Empire. When the time comes to field its armies, he will be at their head, urging them onward as he decapitates an enemy with each swing of his macahuitl.

Profile: Four Jaguar

Corporeal: D:3d10, N:3d12, S:4d10, Q:3d6, V:3d8

Climbin' 2d12, dodge 3d12, fightin': macahuitl 6d12, sneak 3d12, throwin': Aztec magic, balanced 5d10

Mental: C:2d8, K:2d6, M:3d10, Sm:3d6, Sp:2d10

Academia: occult, Aztec culture and lore 4d6, faith 4d10, guts 4d10, Nahuatl 4d6, Spanish 2d6, English 1d6, leadership 5d10, overawe 4d10, scrutinize 3d8, search 3d8, survival: desert, mountains 4d6, trackin' 2d6, trade: farming 4d6

Wind: 18

Edges: Arcane background: Aztec 3, brawny 3, good birth omens 5, thick-skinned 3

Hindrances: Blood sacrifice -2, enemy (Priests of Quetzalcoatl) -5, intolerance ("Spaniards") -3, self-righteous -3, superstitious -2, yearnin' (retake Mexico for Aztecs) -5

Special Abilities:

Black magic: animal mastery 3, bolts o' doom 3, cloak o' evil 2, darts of mixcoatl 3, forewarnin' 2, involuntary sacrifice 2, jaguar's swiftness 4, obsidian winds 2, skin of the pimply one 3, spook 3

Description: Four Jaguar is a big, broad-shouldered Aztec with a kindly face which turns to sneering hatred at the thought or mention of the Spaniards. In battle he wears an elaborate war suit, complete with jaguar skin and eagle feathers, and he paints his face black, gold, and blue to emulate his patron deity, Huitzilopochtli.

Seven Vulture

In almost complete contrast to Four Jaguar, Seven Vulture is a scrawny, crafty old man who's seen more years than any Aztec save Xitlan himself. He and his people, many of whom are skilled craftsmen and obsidian workers, live in Chicometlacalli, a network of caves in an almost inaccessible canyon in the northwestern part of the central plateau of Mexico. Since their home provides few places where they can grow corn or other vegetables, they must trade their handmade goods to other Aztec communities for food. This means risk, since outsiders could detect a trade caravan of porters and follow it back to the settlement.

Therefore the leaders of Chicometlacalli must enforce many security measures to keep the place safe from Spaniards. Seven Vulture punishes transgressors with an iron hand. Anyone who compromises the security of the community almost certainly finds himself stretched over the altar stone, offering his heart to the gods in recompense for his failure. Seven Vulture, a harsh, didactic, and authoritarian ruler, seems to enjoy applying this—and other—punishments.

Although a devout worshipper of the gods, and a skilled priest, Seven Vulture only pays lip service to the notion and goals of the Secret Empire. While he would always welcome more power, he thinks the idea of taking on the Spaniards is folly and will lead the Aztec communities to ruin. He's perfectly content to remain where he is, ruling his own little domain with as little regard for the outside world as possible.

Seven Vulture's patron god is Mictlantecuhtli, god of the dead, He serves as chief priest for all major ceremonies at the hidden Temple of

Mictlantecuhtli which the Secret Empire maintains in the northern desert. Death and dying obsess Seven Vulture, and he takes any opportunity to study them. He would dearly like to learn how to cheat death as Xitlan has done, but the Green Feather Emperor has refused to part with any of his secrets. Seven Vulture would no doubt be gratified to learn that the Reckoners plan to send him back Harrowed after he dies.

Profile: Seven Vulture

Corporeal: D:2d6, N:2d6, S:2d6, Q:3d6, V:2d6

Climbin' 1d6, dodge 2d6, fightin': macahuitl 1d6, sneak 5d6, throwin': Aztec magic 5d6

Mental: C:3d10, K:3d8, M:4d8, Sm:2d8, Sp:2d12

Academia: occult 3d8, academia: Aztec culture and lore 4d8, faith 3d12, guts 3d12, Nahuatl 4d8, Spanish 2d8, leadership 3d8, overawe 4d8, scrutinize 3d10, search 2d10, survival (mountains) 4d8

Wind: 18

Edges: Arcane background: Aztec 3, eagle eyes 1, "the stare" 1

Hindrances: Enemy (Priests of Quetzalcoatl) -5, intolerance ("Spaniards") -3, scrawny -5, self-righteous -3, superstitious -2, yearnin' (to cheat death) -3

Special Abilities:
  Black Magic: create nagual 3, dark protection 4, darts of mixcoatl 2, forewarnin' 2, jaguar's swiftness 2, nahual 2, obsidian winds 3, pact 3, spook 2, stun 4, sun of the jaguar 3
Description: Seven Vulture's name was well chosen—he looks like a scrawny old vulture all dressed up to go to a costume party. He's bald, and his skin is pale from years of living in caves. He wears the elaborate robes of an Aztec ruler, only putting them aside for the skull-and-bones regalia of Mictlantecuhtli when he must.

Twelve Motion

One of the Aztec farming communities with which Chicometlacalli trades is located to the west, hidden in the forests of a remote stretch of coast near Guadalajara. Its leader, a powerful priest-sorcerer named Twelve Motion, serves Xipe Totec, the god of spring. Most of his people offer special veneration to the Flayed Lord as well, to ensure the fertility of their fields. To make sure they continue to have excellent harvests, they have established

an elaborate series of rituals to propitiate Xipe, most of which involve flaying a captive alive as a sacrifice.

Bands of the village's most skilled warriors travel to regions of the country where Spaniards live, find a likely victim, and kidnap him (if you wish to have the posse encounter one of these hunting groups, use the typical Aztec Warrior profile on page 106, but increase *sneak* to 5d8). After the victim arrives in the village, he becomes the focus of a ceremony in which he first takes the place of the god, then becomes a sacrifice to him.

Twelve Motion strips the skin from the victim's flesh with the ease of long practice and wears it as a garment until it falls to pieces. Then he buries the pieces in the village's fields. (If you want a hook to steer your posse toward this settlement, you may wish to have the flayed skins knit themselves back together and become Aztec-hunting abominations, Marshal.)

Twelve Motion himself represents a sort of Aztec ideal: he's tall, strong, handsome, wise, and knowledgeable. Many in the Secret Empire compare him to Nezahualcoyotl, the philosopher-king of the old city-state of Texcoco.

Although his devotion to Xitlan, whom he worships almost as a god, and to the goals of the Secret Empire is absolute, the Green Feather Emperor actually dislikes and distrusts him. He feels Twelve Motion's popularity throughout the Empire poses a threat to his (Xitlan's) leadership, and he would like to find a way to eliminate him without arousing suspicion. A lesser Lord, Nine Lizard, possesses a jealous hatred of Twelve Motion, and Xitlan may try to trick him into doing the deed.

Profile: Twelve Motion

Corporeal: D:2d8, N:3d10, S:3d8, Q:4d6, V:2d8
Climbin' 1d10, dodge 3d10, fightin': macahuitl, knife 3d10, sneak 3d10, throwin': Aztec magic, balanced 5d8

Mental: C:4d8, K:3d6, M:3d8, Sm:4d6, Sp:3d12
Academia: occult, Aztec culture and lore 4d6, faith 5d12, guts 4d12, Nahuatl 4d6, Spanish 1d6, English 1d6, leadership 5d8, overawe 3d8, scrutinize 4d8, search 3d8, trade: farming 4d6

Wind: 20

Edges: Arcane background: Aztec 3, brave 2, purty 1

Hindrances: Enemy (Priests of Quetzalcoatl) –5, intolerance ("Spaniards") –3, superstitious –2, yearnin' (to retake Mexico for the Aztecs) –5

Special Abilities:

Black Magic: animal mastery 3, cloak o' evil 4, create nagual 2, darts of mixcoatl 3, forewarnin' 3, involuntary sacrifice 2, jaguar's swiftness 1, nahual 2, obsidian winds 3, pact 2, stun 4, sun of the jaguar 3, zombie 2

Description: Normally, the tall and handsome (even to European eyes) 12 Motion wears a simple cotton loincloth with just a few other items indicating his status as priest and ruler. For maximum effect, you may wish to have the posse encounter him not long after a sacrifice to Xipe Totec has been made, when he wears a rotting, bloody human skin as a head-to-toe garment.

Plans and Schemes

A conspiracy that lasts for centuries can spend a lot of time developing its plans. Xitlan and the Lords of the Obsidian Blade have honed their plans until they're as sharp as an *iztli*, though the arrival of the French has forced them to adjust things a bit.

The Secret Empire's scheme presently hinges on Santa Anna's ability to overthrow the French. Initially Xitlan had wanted to strike down the Mexicans in one bloody night of vengeance, but when the French took over, and didn't use as many Indian servants as the Mexicans, he had to rethink that. Before he can put that plan into play, he needs to have Mexicans controlling the country again (as much as it galls him to support the Spaniards in *anything*).

Xitlan knows that Santa Anna still wants to rule Mexico, and has subtly fanned the flames of that desire. However, Santa Anna's army by itself, cannot stand against the French forces. Xitlan has persuaded him to use the French soldiers under his command in ways that will increase their casualties, thus weakening the overall French force (and strengthening the Army of the Dead). He may also try to infect the Frenchmen with Montezuma's Revenge (see page 90) before they return to Mexico City, since he's not worried about any Spaniards that may kill (and he can use his magic to "inoculate" his own spies in the city).

The weakness of the French would give Santa Anna an opportunity to strike against them and take the country back. With the help of the Army of the Dead, his army would have a chance to pull off a coup. Information gathered by Xitlan's spies would help him fend off counterattacks from French forces stationed in other cities (and they, too, might be brought low by pestilence).

Thus, Santa Anna ends up in power—but with a weakened army, and ultimately dependent upon his zombie soldiers. Just at his moment of triumph, Xitlan will pull the rug out from under him, taking away the Army and calling on his Aztec followers to rise up across the land and butcher the Spaniards. Spies long in place as "servants" to prominent Mexicans would kill their "masters" and families, plunging the country into chaos. Entire villages would fall before the Aztec soldiers' obsidian weapons. The Mexican Army, divided, demoralized, and unable to fight the Aztecs effectively on their own turf, would follow them down to Mictlan. Assuming all goes well, within weeks the New Aztec Empire would control Mexico.

This plan appeals to the Reckoners for several reasons. One, the widespread chaos caused by these attacks will certainly cause the Fear Level south o' the border to skyrocket. Two, the enormous number of sacrifices performed by the priests during the bloodbath would cause the peasants to live in abject fear, thereby strengthening them, and thus in turn their servants on Earth. Third, it would eliminate one of the Catholic Church's centers of power, and anything which hampers the blessed helps them. Therefore, they plan to support Xitlan and the Lords of the Obsidian Blade wholeheartedly, offering them as much power as they need to accomplish the second conquest of Mexico.

OTHER ACTIVITIES

Even grand conspiracies such as this are supported by many lesser activities that build and support the conspiracy's framework and weaken its enemies. The soldiers of the Secret Empire are busy throughout Mexico every night, performing acts of sabotage, destruction, and murder raising the fear throughout the countryside and causing as much harm to the enemy as possible.

The following list includes some of their many activities, any one of which could provide a good seed for a south o' the border scenario:

Kidnapping innocent people for use as sacrifices.

Poisoning village wells to cause loss of crops, death, and misery.

Cutting railroad lines, telegraph lines, and the like.

Informing the Mexican army, Juaristas, and Porfiriatistas about each others' movements and plans so that the Spaniards kill each other off, saving the Aztecs the trouble.

Burning crops, houses, and villages.

Defacing churches.

Capturing (or breeding) abominations and setting them loose in settled areas.

Spreading stories to increase the fear, and indirectly their power.

PROFILE: TYPICAL AZTEC WARRIOR

Corporeal: D:2d8, N:3d8, S:3d6, Q:3d6, V:2d6

Climbin' 2d8, dodge 2d8, fightin': macahuitl, spear 3d8, swimmin' 2d8, sneak 2d8

Mental: C:3d6, K:2d6, M:3d6, Sm:2d6, Sp:2d6

Area knowledge (Mexico) 2d6, guts 2d6, Spanish 1d6, Nahuatl 2d6, overawe 2d6, search 3d6, survival: desert, mountains 4d6

Pace: 8

Wind: 18

Edges: Tough as nails 3

Hindrances: Bloodthirsty –2, intolerance (non-Aztecs) –3, oath (bring Lords of Obsidian Blade to power) –5, superstitious (follows Aztec superstitions) –2

Gear: Macahuitl, *ichcauipilli* armor, atlatl, obsidian spear.

RESOURCES

Having worked towards their goal for so long, the Lords of the Obsidian Blade have accumulated a substantial store of resources to help them meet that goal. In addition to racking up Appeasement points with the gods, and collecting sacred Aztec relics (see below), they've got several other things working in their favor.

PLANTAGRITO

As mentioned earlier, the Aztecs grow this Reckoning-spawned plant in large plantations around the ruins of Teotihuacán. In addition to its use in pacifying zombies, it can be processed into a painkilling medicine (albeit one which may cause users to develop a *hankerin'* for more), a mild poison, or several other useful things.

Most of the crop goes to keep the Army of the Dead in line. If the *plantagrito* fields are threatened, the Aztecs (including at least one Lord) fight to the death to protect them, knowing their valiant deeds assure them a place in Heaven if they fall.

GOLD AND SILVER

Although it normally eschews "white man's money" for the traditional Aztec barter system, the Secret Empire recognizes the value of cold, hard cash in the white men's world. Few people are willing to trade for obsidian daggers these days.

Over the centuries Indian slaves have squirreled away plenty of gold and silver nuggets for the Empire's use. If necessary the Empire will hire mercenaries or "independent regulators" to help it meet some of its goals—though the Lords are careful to hide from the heroes who they're really working for, of course.

FEAR

Since ultimately the Lords of the Obsidian Blade serve the Reckoners, high Fear Levels help them, and hinder their enemies. They have worked hard to foster fear as much as possible—for example, by spreading stories about the horrors stalking the Weird West, breeding and feeding abominations, and so forth.

The Reckoners have rewarded the Lords' hard work on their behalf. Whenever an Aztec sorcerer-priest uses a black magic spell which causes damage, add the local Fear Level to the damage roll. Likewise, when using any spell which calls for a contest of Traits, the sorcerer gets a bonus to his roll equal to the Fear Level.

PLACES O' POWER

Many places are sacred to the Lords of the Obsidian Blade, and in these places, their powers work even stronger. In game terms, whenever an Aztec sorcerer-priest uses a favor or casts a black magic spell in one of the areas listed below, add +1 to the roll. The Fear Level bonus described above also applies.

THE TEMPLE OF MICTLANTECUHTLI

Built in an isolated box canyon in the northern desert which Jaguar and Eagle Knights carefully guard, this nine-level temple serves as the chief focus of worship for Mictlantecuhtli, god of the dead. Each of its nine levels represent one of the nine levels of Mictlan that the spirits of dead Aztecs pass through on their way to their final rest. Inside each level of the pyramid, traps fashioned to resemble that stage on the journey through the underworld destroy any intruders who try to penetrate to the final, inner sanctum, where the Aztecs store much treasure.

THE FIELDS OF WAR

Up in the Tlaxcalan highlands, northeast of Mexico City, the Secret Empire built a training ground where promising young Aztec men could learn to become Jaguar and Eagle Knights. Here, the Aztecs learn and practice their arts of war. The Fields also feature a major temple to Huitzilopochtli, god of war.

THE HOUSE OF THE PAINTING OF BOOKS

Within Mexico City itself, the Secret Empire has managed to create several hiding places where it can hold minor rituals and perform other functions, such as processing *plantagrito*. One of

AZTEC BLOOD MAGIC

In order to assist their Aztec servants, the Reckoners have given them special powers known as *blood magic*, or Aztec sorcery. Powered by human sacrifices and similar rituals, blood magic provides the Lords of the Obsidian Blade with a potent weapon available to no one else in the Weird West.

In game terms, blood magic works more or less like black magic. It involves the worship of Aztec gods, not nature spirits. In truth, the Aztec gods worshipped by the Secret Empire are simply the Reckoners and various powerful manitous. The four principal gods—Tezcatlipoca, Huitzilopochtli, Tlaloc, and Xipe Totec—are the Reckoners, and the other gods are manitous with powers related to their role in the Aztec pantheon.

To use blood magic, an Aztec sorcerer-priest must make Foolproof (3) *faith* rolls, just like normal black magicians. However, if they are not in good favor with their gods, this roll becomes harder. Remaining in favor with the Aztec gods requires sacrifices of humans and blood. If an Aztec sorcerer-priest does not perform a blood sacrifice each day, and a full-blown human sacrifice every 20 days, it becomes harder for him to use his powers.

For every day he does not sacrifice at least a little of his own blood, increase the Target Number for the *faith* roll by 1. For every 20 days for which he does not make a proper human sacrifice, increase the Target Number by 3.

Aztec sorcerer-priests can also learn regular black magic spells as well. Many blood magic spells use *throwin': Aztec magic* to determine if they hit the target. If ranged, such spells have a Range Increment of 10.

TRAPPINGS

The Aztec religion, particularly as practiced by the Secret Empire, requires various trappings to perform rituals (and thus cast spells) properly. First and foremost among these are the

these "hideouts" is the House of the Painting of Books, a place where Aztec scholars create the elaborate painted "codices" that record Aztec history and lore.

Anyone who infiltrates or breaks into the House (located in a secret basement of a building owned by a *mestizo* friendly to the Secret Empire's cause) finds a combination scriptorium and library where he can "read" all about the history and plans of the Secret Empire. Of course, since the "writing" is elaborate, often highly symbolical pictures, only characters with *academia: Aztec culture and lore* at level 4 or higher can correctly comprehend everything that the codices say. The house is guarded by 10 Aztec warriors, and an Aztec priest at all times.

sacrificial knives, the flint knife (*tecpatl*) and obsidian knife (*iztli*). Each one is specially created, stored, and "blessed" to remain pure enough for use in sacrifices.

Second, a stone bowl carved with an eagle design is used to store hearts as they are ripped out of sacrificial victims' chests. The bowls are made of stone, and the hearts are often burned within it.

Third, special "vestments" are worn. This clothing varies depending on what god is being worshipped (it is, typically, an Earthly representation of the god and his raiments).

These trappings are used for all Aztec blood magic spells. Additional trappings may be required in each spell's description.

AZTEC BLOOD MAGIC SPELLS

The priest of the Secret Empire have a few new spells bestowed upon them by their dark lords. Your posse had better watch its step!

CREATE NAGUAL

Speed: 1 hour
Duration: Permanent
Range: Touch

Using this spell, a sorcerer-priest can transform a willing subject into a Nagual (see *Rascals, Varmints & Critters*). The spell cannot affect an unwilling subject. Since it takes approximately one hour to accomplish the ceremony needed to make the magic take effect, this spell does not work in combat.

DARTS OF MIXCOATL

Speed: 1
Duration: Instant
Range: 10 yards/level

This spell projects a storm of darts at a single target. The sorcerer-priest may create one dart per level in the spell. Each dart does 1d6 damage per level .

The spell's attack roll is a *throwin': Aztec magic* roll. If the roll succeeds exactly, one dart hits the target. For every raise the caster gets, another dart hits the target.

INVOLUNTARY SACRIFICE

Speed: 2
Duration: Instant
Range: 5 yards/level

Not everyone is as willing as the Lords of the Obsidian Blade and their Aztec followers to give up their blood for the gods. Sometimes, other folks need a little encouragement—and this spell gives it to them.

The spell's attack roll is a *throwin': Aztec magic* roll. If it succeeds, the victim's blood bursts from his pores, oozing down over the rest of his body in a crimson shower. The victim takes 1d8 damage per level the caster has in the spell to the guts (armor does not reduce this damage at all), and onlookers have to make an Onerous (7) *guts* check to keep from losing their lunch at this horrible sight.

JAGUAR'S SWIFTNESS

Speed: 1
Duration: 1 round + (1 round/level)
Range: Touch

This spell imbues the caster (or recipient) with the speed and swiftness of the jaguar. For every 5 points the caster gets on his roll, the subject's *Quickness* is increased by 1 die type. If the die type is increased above a d12, each additional level adds +2 to the Trait.

NAHUAL

Speed: 1 minute
Duration: 10 minutes/level
Range: Self

A *nahual* is a god's animal disguise. Each god has a specific animal associated with it whose form it can assume. Using this favor, the shaman can assume that form as well (in fact, the term *nahual* is often used to mean "sorcerer"). Check out the Nahual Table to see which animal forms are associated with a particular Aztec god.

NAHUALS

God	Nahual
Coatlicue	Serpent
Huehuecoyotl	Coyote
Huitzilopochtli	Hummingbird, eagle
Mictlantecuhtli	Owl, bat, spider
Mixcoatl	Deer
Quetzalcoatl	Feathered serpent
Tezcatlipoca	Jaguar, turkey
Tlaloc	Serpent
Tlazolteotl	Cipactli
Xipe Totec	Spoon bird
Xiuhcoatl	Fire serpent (use Mexican dragon, *Rascals, Varmints & Critters*)

OBSIDIAN WINDS

Speed: 2
Duration: Instant
Range: 10 yards/level

The fifth level of the Aztec underworld features a plain where freezing winds tear at the deceased's flesh like obsidian knives. This spell allows a brief gust of that wind out into Anahuac to destroy a sorcerer-priest's foe. The sorcerer-priest makes a *throwin': Aztec magic* roll. If he succeeds, the victim takes damage based on the spell's level.

Obsidian winds affects not only corporeal beings, but incorporeal ones such as ghosts, *tzitzimime*, and the like. However, it cannot damage inanimate objects, such as walls.

Level	Damage
1	2d6
2	3d8
3	4d10
4	5d12
5	6d20

SKIN OF THE PIMPLY ONE

Speed: 1
Duration: 1d6+2 rounds
Range: 5 yards/level

When a sorcerer-priest uses this favor to attack a character, he must make an Opposed *Spirit* roll against his target, adding his level in the spell to his roll. If he wins, the victim's skin becomes covered with pimples, warts, boils, and the like—just like the skin of Nanahuatzin, the god of skin diseases. This reduces the victim's *Deftness, Nimbleness,* and *Mien* die types by 1 for 1d6+2 rounds.

This spell also has a more insidious effect. Anyone who fall victim to this spell must make a Hard (9) *Vigor* roll when the curse expires. Failing the roll means that the change was permanent. The unfortunate hero gains the *ugly as sin* Hindrance. Only the *lay on hands* miracle cast against a Hard (9) TN or the original Aztec priest who cast the spell can remove this affliction.

SUN OF THE JAGUAR

Speed: 2
Duration: Instant
Range: 5 yards/level

This terrifying spell summons up spirit jaguars who rip the target character to shreds, just like the jaguars who killed everyone when the First World came to an end. The spirit jaguars cannot be seen, but their effects—terrible claw and bite marks—are clearly visible, as is a loud growling. There is nothing the unfortunate victim can do to defend himself.

The attack roll for *sun of the jaguar* is a *throwin': Aztec magic* roll versus a TN of 5 plus the victim's *fightin': brawlin'*. The damage caused depends on the spell's level.

Level	Damage
1	5d6
2	5d8
3	5d10
4	5d12
5	5d20

Aztec Relics

In addition to their blood magic, the Lords of the Obsidian Blade also have a collection of powerful Aztec relics. Some of the items in it are described below. Of course, you can always decided that one of these relics isn't in their possession yet—it was lost centuries ago and they're still looking for it. Guess what the posse just found?

Blood Iztli

When the Aztecs sacrificed 20,000 people to dedicate their Great Temple in 1487, four specially consecrated *iztlis* were used for the gruesome task. All four of them have survived, and two are in the possession of the Lords of the Obsidian Blade. The others remain lost; heaven knows what evil they could inspire if found by the wrong persons.

Power: A Blood Iztli can be used in combat as a normal knife doing STR+2d6 damage. It does not remain bloody after use, though—any blood on the blade is quickly "sucked" inside it, a horrible sight which requires an Onerous (7) *guts* checks.

A Blood Iztli also aids Aztec blood magic. Any *human sacrifice, maim,* or *scar* rituals performed using it net the user +1 Appeasement.

Taint: Anyone who possesses a Blood Iztli becomes *bloodthirsty.* If already *bloodthirsty,* the possessor becomes *mean as a rattler* as well.

Feathered Cloak

Aztec lords often wore headdresses or garments sewn with feathers in every color of the rainbow, which were bartered from tribes living in the southern jungles. Sometimes priests of Quetzalcoatl would imbue a feathered cloak with the power of their god in his role as Ehécatl, god of the wind, so that its wearer could fly like the birds who supplied the feathers.

Power: A Feathered Cloak provides the wearer with the ability to fly at Pace 10.

Taint: Typically none. Some cloaks inflict an *intolerance* of Tezcatlipoca worshippers on their wearers, but this is rare.

Jaguar Skin

Said to be enchanted by Tezcatlipoca himself, this lush animal pelt, when wrapped around a character's body, allows him to change his shape into that of a jaguar.

Power: The character's body transforms into a jaguar. Use the Corporeal Traits and *Mien* for the Mountain Lion (see *The Marshal's Handbook*), but let the character keep his other normal Mental Traits. The character can change his shape back at any time.

Taint: After a transformation, the wearer has a strong craving for raw meat. Failure to eat some meat (at least a half pound) causes 2d6 damage to the guts.

SCEPTRE OF MICTLANTECUHTLI

Carved from human bone, this sceptre resembles the one sometimes carried by the god of the dead. It possesses a lesser version of the power that his sceptre has—to strike dead anyone whom it touches.

Power: Anyone touched with the Sceptre (this usually requires a *fightin'* roll) takes 3d10 damage to the guts. The Sceptre may only be used 9 times a day.

Taint: Anyone who carries the Sceptre becomes a *grim servant o' death*.

SMOKING MIRROR

A gift to the Aztecs from their god Tezcatlipoca, this mirror of obsidian possesses the power to show the future to those wise enough to use it. Whether that future is fixed, or merely one possible outcome, is up to you.

Power: The user must make a Hard (9) *Spirit* roll. If he succeeds, the darkness on the face of the mirror parts to show him a glimpse of the future. It may not be what he wanted to see—that requires at least one raise on the *Spirit* roll—but it displays some significant event of the not-too-distant future (within, say, one year). The mirror can only be used once every 20 days.

Taint: None.

XIUHCOATL

A lesser form of the weapon carried by Huitzilopochtli and Xiuhtecuhtli, the Xiuhcoatl—"Fire Serpent"—is the most potent weapon in the Aztec arsenal. It projects a devastating blast of flame which can kill people, destroy buildings, and set just about anything on fire.

Power: The Xiuhcoatl can emit a blast of flame nine times a day. Each blast does 6d10 damage, and has a Range Increment of 20.

Taint: The character develops a minor *yearnin'* to use the Xiuhcoatl, and to set fires in general.

PRIESTS OF THE FEATHERED SERPENT

For every conspiracy, there's a counter-conspiracy. In this case, the Lords of the Obsidian Blade, devotees of the sorcerer god Tezcatlipoca, are opposed by the priests of their god's ancient enemy, Quetzalcoatl, the Plumed Serpent, god of wisdom, knowledge, and the wind.

Even when the Spaniards were still enslaving the Aztecs, and treating them with great cruelty, there were some among the Aztec leaders who believed that the two peoples could, and should, learn to live together. They did not want to destroy the Spaniards, or to convert them to the Aztec way of life, but merely to figure out how to co-exist with them. They wanted to be left alone to live their lives as they wished, and let the white men do the same. There was little hope for such a dream then, and not much more hope now—but they remain determined to try.

Unfortunately, the odds are stacked against them. Their numbers are slight, and their message appeals to far fewer Aztecs than the creed of hate, revenge, and violence preached by the Lords of the Obsidian Blade. Since their god does not want human sacrifices, they lack a counterpart for the Lords' enormous favors from the dark gods. The fact that many of them are *pacifists* doesn't help matters. If they're going to oppose the Lords effectively, they're probably going to have to combine their resources with those of some other group—say, the posse.

SIX WIND

The leader of the Priests is an old priest named, aptly enough, Six Wind. Although he's getting on in years, he's still pretty spry, and his faith is strong. His main responsibility now is to pass on his knowledge and wisdom to the other priests, and to his people. He knows he doesn't have much time left, so he takes every opportunity he can to impart his knowledge to those around him.

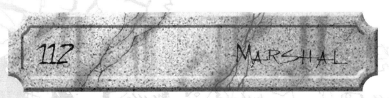

Several underpriests serve Six Wind directly in various capacities. They include Two Dog, the closest thing the Priests have to a "War Chief"; Four House, a skilled calendar-keeper and spellcaster; Thirteen Rabbit, a very popular priest who seems very likely to succeed Six Wind; and Ten Flower, a close friend and ally of two Dog.

Unlike the Lords of the Obsidian Blade, who suffer from rivalries and hatred among themselves, the Priests of Quetzalcoatl, from highest to lowest, remain united in their goals, desires, and philosophies. Their single-mindedness and strength of purpose in opposing the Lords constitutes, perhaps, their greatest strength.

PROFILE: SIX WIND

Corporeal: D:2d6, N:2d6, S:2d6, Q:3d6, V:2d6

Climbin' 1d6, dodge 2d6, fightin': macahuitl 2d6, sneak 3d6

Mental: C:4d10, K:3d8, M:4d8, Sm:2d8, Sp:4d10

Academia: occult, Aztec culture and lore 6d8, faith 6d10, guts 4d10, Nahuatl 4d8, Spanish 2d8, leadership 3d8, overawe 3d8, scrutinize 2d10, search 2d10, survival (mountains) 4d8

Wind: 16

Edges: Arcane background: Aztec 3, good birth omens 3

Hindrances: All thumbs –2, blood sacrifice –2, enemy (Secret Empire) –3, Old Ways vow –3, pacifist –3, superstitious –2

Special Abilities:

  Ritual 4: Fast, maim, paint, peyote, pledge, scar

  Favors: Call weather (Tlaloc's blessing), healing (Patecatl's touch), heal madness, lightning strike (Tlaloc's dart), turtle's shell

Description: 6 Wind is an old Aztec priest, his skin a deep, wrinkled brown from years of exposure to the sun. He is almost completely bald. Despite his apparent infirmity, he remains in good health and strong enough to walk, run, use favors, and oppose his hated enemies, the Secret Empire. He longs for a way for Spaniards and Aztecs to live together, but sees little hope of this ever happening.

THE TEMPLE OF THE WINDS

Compared to the Lords of the Obsidian Blade, the Priests of Quetzalcoatl have relatively few resources to call on. Their people number less than a thousand, most living in tiny villages of no more than 50 located in hidden forests and valleys in the mountains.

The Priests' "headquarters," if they have one at all, is the Temple of the Winds, a centuries-old sacred site built in the unexplored wilderness of northern Veracruz state. Like many temples to Quetzalcoatl, it is round instead of square. Any favor used here by a priests has its Appeasement cost reduced by –1 (minimum cost of 1 Appeasement).

Abominations Appendix

Brimstone Men

The "superstitious locals" whom Bascomb dismisses aren't entirely off the mark. The volcanoes aren't likely to erupt anytime soon—provided the Aztecs don't mess with 'em—but people *have* been seeing Brimstone Men. These fiends, created by the Reckoners to exploit human fears of volcanoes and fire, and regarded by the Aztec sorcerers as the warrior-servants of Xiuhtecuhtli, live in the hearts of the Mexican volcanoes (primarily Popocatépetl and Itzacíhuatl). Occasionally they worm their way out through cracks and fissures into the "cold world" and try to snatch an unwary sulfur miner or farmer as a quick snack.

Profile: Hombre de Azufre (Brimstone Man)

Corporeal: D:3d8, N:3d8, S:4d10, Q:3d6, V:4d8
Climbin' 3d8, dodge 3d8, fightin': brawlin' 4d8, sneak 3d8
Mental: C:2d6, K:3d4, M:3d8, Sm:2d6, Sp:2d6
Overawe 3d8
Pace: 6
Size: 6
Wind: 14
Terror: 9
Special Abilities:
> **Lava Form:** Brimstone Men are made of lava and red-hot rock. This form grants them Armor 2 against all attacks.
> **Fiery Touch:** If a Brimstone Man succeeds in touching someone (*i.e.,* makes a successful *fightin': brawlin'* roll), the target takes STR+4d8 damage from the creature's burning touch. Any flammable objects on the victim,

such as clothes, catch fire (see *The Weird West Player's Guide* for more info on fire damage).

> **Vulnerability to water:** Brimstone Men take 2d8 damage for every canteen full of water thrown on them. Anyone within 2 yards of a Brimstone Man when it gets doused takes 2d6 damage from the super-heated steam coming off of its body.
> **Coup:** Counting coup on a Brimstone Men nets a Harrowed the *hell fire* power at level 1.

Description: A humanoid creature seemingly made of red-hot rock covered with a network of cracks which ooze lava. It smells of, naturally, brimstone.

The San Patricio Battalion

Not all Americans fought the Mexicans loyally during the war. A group of them, about half of whom were Irish, defected to the Mexican side and were formed into the San Patricio (St. Patrick) Battalion. After the war they were captured and court-martialed for desertion. Those who were not shot or hung were whipped, branded with a "D," and turned loose.

These survivors now roam the badlands of the Confederacy and the northern half of Mexico in loose gangs of desperate men. Lacking any friends or loyalties, other than to themselves, they rob, rape, and murder. The chaotic situation in Mexico, and Confederate attention to the War Between the States, has prevented anyone from going after them in force. Substantial rewards are offered for them, though.

Although most of the San Patricios are getting old, they're tough from years of living a life of banditry in the wilderness. A few who have died have come back Harrowed.

Profile: San Patricios

Corporeal: D:2d10, N:3d10, S:3d6, Q:3d8, V:3d8
Climbin' 1d10, dodge 3d10, fightin': brawlin' 2d10, horse ridin' 2d10, quick draw: pistol 3d8, shootin': pistol, rifle 2d10

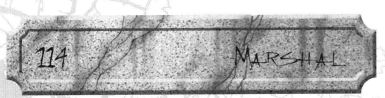

MARSHAL

Mental: C:3d6, K:2d6, M:2d8, Sm:2d6, Sp:2d6

Area knowledge (Texas) 2d6, artillery: cannons 1d6, guts 3d6, English 2d6, Spanish 1d6, overawe 2d8, search 2d6, trackin' 2d6

Pace: 10

Wind: 14

Edges: Varies, but typically includes *nerves o' steel, tough as nails,* and *"the stare."*

Hindrances: Intolerant (Americans) –3, mean as a rattler –2, outlaw –3, vengeful –3

Gear: Various pistols, knives, etc.; horse and tack.

Vinegarroons

The ordinary vinegarroon scorpions which Bascomb described are bad enough, though he exaggerates their size and the quickness of their poison a bit. But he's never run into one of the *really* big ones—the giant-sized scorps which'll give your posse nightmares.

Giant vinegarroons live in deep canyons and caves throughout the Sonora Desert. They're as fast as horses (at least for short distances), have claws which grip like iron, and a poison-coated stinger big enough to drive an arm-sized hole through a man's chest—all in all not something to tangle with lightly.

Profile: Vinegarroons

Corporeal: D:2d6, N:3d6, S:1d4, Q:2d8, V:1d4

Fightin': brawlin' 3d6

Mental: C:1d4, K:1d4, M:1d4, Sm:1d4, Sp:1d4

Pace: 6

Size: 1

Wind: 8

Terror: 3

Special Abilities:

Claws: 1 point of Wind damage when able to pinch exposed flesh.

Sting: The vinegarroon's sting does 1 point of Wind damage to exposed flesh. If the victim takes damage from the sting, venom is injected into the wound. The venom does a total of 6d6 damage to the guts, applied in 1d6 increments for six rounds. The pain from the poison is so intense that all of the victim's Corporeal Trait die types are reduced by 1 if he tries to do anything.

Description: A pale brown to dark yellowish arthropod with two pincers, six other legs, and a tail with a stinger.

without having to roll to hit or take an action. An opposed *Strength* roll is needed to break free.

Sting: STR+1d6

Venom: If the Sting does damage, a giant vinegarroon injects venom into the victim. This works like normal vinegarroon venom, but does 12d6 damage (2d6 per round for six rounds), and the pain penalty is doubled.

BARRANCA PROWLER

Another abomination found in the Copper Canyon area (and elsewhere throughout northern Mexico) is known as the barranca prowler (or, to some peasants, *el gato del diablo*—the Devil's cat). It lairs in caves and abandoned mines, and feeds off of whatever it can catch. It seems to find the taste of human flesh particularly succulent.

Barranca prowlers have adapted well to their environment. They are extremely stealthy, using their natural grace and appearance to blend into the rocks. If necessary, they can climb like a mountain goat. Sometimes it almost seems like they can run right up a bare rock face! One of the creature's favorite tactics is to ambush a group of people, snatch one of them, and carry him up a cliff side to a position where the victim's friends can't rescue him. Then it enjoys a leisurely meal.

PROFILE: GIANT VINEGARROON

Corporeal: D:3d8, N:3d10, S:4d12+4, Q:3d10, V:4d8

Fightin': brawlin' 4d10

Mental: C:1d6, K:1d6, M:2d6, Sm:1d6, Sp:1d4

Overawe 6d6

Pace: 18

Size: 10-15

Wind: 12

Terror: 11

Special Abilities:

Armor: The giant vinegarroon's tough carapace gives it 2 points of Armor.

Claws: STR+1d8. After a successful hit, the giant vinegarroon can maintain its grip on the victim, doing STR damage each action

PROFILE: BARRANCA PROWLER

Corporeal: D:2d8, N:2d10, S:3d12, Q:3d8, V:4d6

Climbin' 5d8, fightin': brawlin' 4d10, sneak 5d10

Mental: C:2d6, K:1d6, M:2d6, Sm:1d6, Sp:1d4

Overawe 4d6

Pace: 10

Size: 5

Wind: 10

Terror: 7

Special Abilities:

Armor: The barranca prowler's rocky skin gives it 2 points of Armor.

Armor-piercing: The creature's razor-sharp, rock-hard teeth and claws give attacks made with them an AP 2 rating.

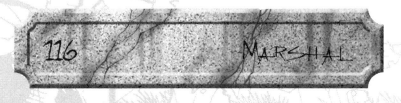

Bite: STR+2d6

Camouflage: The prowler's rocky appearance grants it a +6 to all *sneak* rolls made while in the canyons.

Claws: STR+2d6

Description: A barranca prowler looks sort of like an emaciated sabertooth tiger made out of scabrous red rock resembling the canyon walls.

Los Diablitos

The Reckoners sometimes use the spirits of bulls slain in the bullring to make *Los Diablitos* ("the Little Devils"). They use these to torment up-and-coming heroes. Any hero who's accumulated three or four points of Grit may have one of these sent after him in the hopes of polishing him off early, without having to risk a Los Diablos. Anyone who encounters one of these creatures can be sure she's attracted the attention of the Reckoners.

Los Diablitos aren't nearly as powerful or as frightening as Los Diablos, of course, but the Reckoners often wait to send them out until their quarry is already injured or in desperate straits. Once a Diablito kills its victim (or a person it is distracted into attacking; see below) or is killed, it vanishes in a puff of dark, sulfurous smoke.

Profile: Los Diablitos

Corporeal: D:1d4, N:1d8, S:3d12+2, Q:2d8, V:1d12

Fightin': brawlin' 4d8, sneak 2d8, swimmin' 1d8

Mental: C:2d8, K:1d4, M:2d10, Sm:1d6, Sp:1d8

Overawe 3d10

Pace: 10

Size: 8

Wind: 20

Terror: 7

Special Abilities:

Armor: 1

Horns: STR+1d10

Seein' Red: Los Diablitos can be distracted by other persons wearing red clothing. If someone within 20 feet of their intended victim is wearing a red shirt, pants, skirt, jacket, or similarly-sized

piece of clothing, a Diablito must make a Fair (5) *Spirit* roll or attack that person instead. Once the new victim is dead, it returns to its original target.

Description: A Diablito looks like a big, mean, ugly bull with especially large, sharp horns. Two or three two-foot-long metal spikes are stuck point-first into his neck, but don't seem to hamper his ability to move his head and neck any.

Aztec Abominations

The following abominations from Aztec mythology arose following the Reckoning in 1863. Many have come about due to the actions of the Lords of the Obsidian Blade. The posse might encounter most of these creatures just about anywhere in Mexico.

Cipactli

Cipactli, the earth monster, has a central role in Aztec myth. According to legend, she bit off Tezcatlipoca's missing foot during the same conflict in which he tore off her lower jaw to form the earth.

Posse members might encounter Cipactli, an Aztec myth brought to life by the power of the Reckoning, in just about any swamp or lake. A Fearmonger, she spreads terror and dread for miles around her, raising an area's Fear Level by at least one or two points.

Cipactli resembles a sort of cross between a crocodile and a toad (though she favors the croc). Short, sharp spines cover much of her body. She lacks a lower jaw, so she can only smash targets with her sharp upper teeth rather than actually bite them. At each of her joints there is a mouth, each filled with sharp teeth and constantly dripping blood.

Although not especially fast or dextrous, Cipactli is immensely strong and larger than the longest Mojave rattler. Her thick hide protects her from most damage. Any posse which manages to defeat her gains the satisfaction of defeating a major Fearmonger—including a point of Grit.

Cipactli also has "children"—lesser versions of herself who inhabit other lakes and swamps. Although not as fearsome as their parent, Cipactli's children can still be a handful.

PROFILE: CIPACTLI

Corporeal: D:2d6, N:2d6, S:6d12+20, Q:1d6, V:4d12+8
Fightin': brawlin' 10d6, swimmin' 8d6
Mental: C:3d8, K:3d6, M:4d12+8, Sm:2d8, Sp:4d10
Overawe 5d12+8
Pace: 12 running/20 swimming
Size: 25
Wind: NA
Terror: 13
Special Abilities:
 Armor: 3
 Teeth: STR+2d10
 Spines: Anyone punching, brushing up against, or even just touching, Cipactli suffers 1d8 damage to the affected area from her spines.
 Mouths: Cipactli's joint-mouths can bite for STR damage.
Description: See text.

PROFILE: CIPACTLI'S CHILDREN

Corporeal: D:2d6, N:2d8, S:3d12+4, Q:2d6, V:3d12
Fightin': brawlin' 5d8, swimmin' 5d6
Mental: C:2d6, K:1d6, M:3d12, Sm:1d6, Sp:3d8
Overawe 4d12
Pace: 8 running/10 swimming
Size: 10
Wind: 24
Terror: 9
Special Abilities:
 Armor: 2
 Teeth: STR+1d10
 Spines: Anyone punching, brushing up against, or even just touching one of Cipactli's Children suffers 1d6 damage to the affected area from her spines.
 Mouths: Cipactli's Children's joint-mouths bite for STR damage.
Description: See text.

CIHUATETEO

The ghostly spirits of women who died in childbirth, cihuateteo seek vengeance on mankind. Filled with rage and hate, they try to harm humans, particularly children and handsome men.

They have the power to inflict diseases and deformities such as strokes, palsy, harelip, a clubfoot,

spasms, and similar problems upon their victims. In order to keep them at bay, people offer prayers to them at shrines dedicated to them, and at crossroads.

PROFILE: CHUATETEO

Corporeal: D:3d8, N:3d10, S:2d6, Q:4d8, V:3d8

Dodge 3d10, fightin': brawlin' 4d10

Mental: C:2d6, K:1d6, M:3d10, Sm:1d6, Sp:3d8

Pace: 10

Size: 6

Wind: 16

Terror: 7

Special Abilities:

Flight: Pace 15.

Inflict Disease/Deformity: With a successful *fightin': brawlin'* roll, a cihuateteo can inflict the sorts of illnesses and deformities described above. Represent these conditions with various Hindrances, such as *ailin', bad ears, bad eyes, lame, one-armed bandit,* or *scrawny*.

Propitiation: Cihuateteo suffer a –2 penalty on *fightin'* rolls to hit anyone who has offered a prayer to them within the past 24 hours.

Undead.

Description: Cihuateteo resemble young women with long black hair and skull-like faces. They wear long skirts and headdresses. Their flesh has the pallor and stink of death, and their breasts sag horrifically.

FEATHERED SERPENT

This fabulous beast, the *nahualli* of Quetzalcoatl, is a snake with feathers. Along its head and spine, it has blue-green feathers similar to those of the quetzal bird; the feathers taper down to a long tail. Along its bottom it has reddish scales.

Feathered serpents can fly. They use this ability to swoop down on prey (including humans) and bite them with its poisonous fangs.

PROFILE: FEATHERED SERPENT

Corporeal: D:2d8, N:2d8, S:2d6, Q:3d8, V:2d8

Dodge 3d8, fightin': brawlin' 4d8

Mental: C:2d6, K:1d6, M:3d8, Sm:1d6, Sp:1d6

Pace: 8

Size: 5

Wind: 14

Terror: 5

Special Abilities:

Bite: STR+1d4

Flight: Pace 10

Venom: Anyone who takes damage from a feathered serpent's bite suffers from its venom as well. The victim must make a Hard (9) *Vigor* roll. If he succeeds, he takes 1d8 damage to the guts, but that's it. If he fails, he takes 1d8 damage to the guts per round for the next 1d8+2 rounds. Armor offers no protection against this damage.

Description: See text.

Pace: 1 (ground)/10 (air)
Size: 3
Wind: 10
Terror: 5
Special Abilities:
   Beak: STR
   Talons: STR+1d6
   Flight: Pace 10
   Night Vision: A Mictlan owl can see as well at night as a human can in the daytime.
   Intolerance For Light: Bright lights, even as much as a single lantern's light, disturb and blind Mictlan owls. They flee from such lights in most cases. If extremely hungry, they may keep attacking, but at –2 to all rolls.
   Screech: Anyone who hears a Mictlan owl screech must make an Onerous (7) *Vigor* roll. Characters who succeed take 2d4 damage to the guts; characters who fail take 6d6 damage to the guts. An owl can only screech this way once every three rounds.
Description: See text.

Night Ax

One of the most fearsome demons in Aztec lore, Night Ax stalks the forests and fields of Mexico at night, seeking victims whose hearts it can rip out and eat.

Profile: Night Ax

Corporeal: D:4d10, N:4d10, S:4d10, Q:4d10, V:4d10
Dodge 4d10, fightin': brawlin' 4d10
Mental: C:4d8, K:4d8, M:4d12, Sm:4d8, Sp:4d8
Overawe 6d12
Pace: 10
Size: 6
Wind: 18
Terror: 11
Special Abilities:
   Immunity: Night Ax is immune to all non-obsidian weapons.
   Claws: STR+1d6
   Heartripping: Night Ax can make a *fightin': brawlin'* roll to grab a hold of a character. Unless that character frees himself before Night Ax gets another action (this requires victory in an Opposed

Mictlan Owl

One of the reasons why the Aztecs regard owls as such bad omens, and associate them with the god of death, is this creature. It resembles a large owl whose jet-black feathers are tipped with red and whose eyes hold a demonic gleam. Its beak and claws are fearsome enough weapons, but its screech can kill anyone who hears it! Fortunately, Mictlan owls are solitary creatures.

Profile: Mictlan Owl

Corporeal: D:1d6, N:2d6, S:1d6, Q:2d6, V:2d6
Dodge 2d6, fightin': brawlin' 4d6, sneak 4d6
Mental: C:2d6, K:1d4, M:2d6, Sm:1d6, Sp:1d4

MARSHAL

Strength roll—good luck), Night Ax tries to rip out his heart. This does 6d10 damage to the victim's gizzards. Night Ax keeps trying until he's got the heart (*i.e.*, the victim's dead) or someone distracts him with some other attack. After he gets a heart, Night Ax takes an action to gobble it down.

Gruesomeness: His appearance requires anyone who sees him to make an Onerous (7) *guts* check each round for the first 1d4 rounds.

Description: Night Ax looks like a headless man with blood pouring from the stump of its neck. In its chest there's a gaping wound where its heart should be. This wound opens and closes periodically with a sound like an ax biting into a tree (hence his name). Below this wound its ribs become clearly visible. When the wind blows, they clack together like macabre wind chimes.

Obsidian Knife Spirits

Not all victims of the sacrificial knife went peacefully to the Aztec heavens. Some died with anger in their hearts. Since the Reckoning, their phantoms have returned to plague the living, wishing to steal from men what they themselves lost so long ago.

Stealthy as a whisper and quick as lightning, these terrible beings, known as obsidian knife spirits, haunt areas where sacrifices took place (primarily Mexico City) and prey on people. They only hunt at night, as they dislike sunlight.

Profile: Obsidian Knife Spirits

Corporeal: D:3d10, N:4d10, S:3d6, Q:4d10, V:2d6

Dodge 4d10, fightin': brawlin' 6d10, stealth 6d10

Mental: C:3d6, K:2d4, M:2d10, Sm:3d6, Sp:2d6

Overawe 4d10

Pace: 10 (ground)/10 (air)

Size: 6

Wind: 12

Terror: 7

Special Abilities:

Immunity: To Wind or physical damage.

Spectral Claws: STR+2d6

Flight: Pace 10

Phantom Form: Obsidian knife spirits are intangible, able to pass through walls, sink into the ground, and move their ghostly hands through some hombre's chest. They cannot take damage from physical weapons or attacks, unless the weapons are made of flint, gold, or jade (though their claws are perfectly capable of hurting corporeal characters). Hexes, miracles, and enchanted weapons can also hurt them.

Aztec Death: Obsidian knife spirits receive a +1 bonus on all rolls (including damage rolls) made against Aztec characters.

Description: An obsidian knife spirit has a vaguely humanoid shape, though its arms seem oddly elongated and its legs trail away to mist and vapor. It looks black and glassy, like the obsidian knife that took its life, and its fingers are long, wickedly sharp claws. Its eyes and mouth are barely visible as slight depressions in its otherwise featureless face.

Tzitzimime

According to Aztec legends, the *tzitzimime* ("those who fell head-first") are female star-demons. When the Fifth Sun comes to an end and the world is about to be destroyed by earthquakes, the tzitzimime will descend to Earth, take the form of jaguars and other beasts, and devour all of mankind. Since

the Reckoning, some of them have taken to coming down ahead of schedule. The Lords of the Obsidian Blade also know special ceremonies (i.e. the *pact* spell) to summon them and loose them on their (the Lords') hated foes.

Profile: Tzitzimime

Corporeal: D:3d10, N:4d12, S:3d10, Q:4d10, V:4d10

Dodge 3d12, fightin': brawlin' 6d12, sneak 5d12

Mental: C:4d10, K:3d8, M:4d12, Sm:2d8, Sp:4d10

Overawe 6d12, scrutinize 4d10, search 4d10

Pace: 12

Size: 6

Wind: NA

Terror: 9

Special Abilities:

　Claws: STR+1d6

　Skeletal Mouths: STR

　Skeletal Eyes: Thanks to its many sets of unblinking eyes, a tzitzimime can see in all directions around itself. Its Target Number for surprise checks can never be higher than Foolproof (3).

　Rattlesnake Privates: Despite the fact that they're considered to be a female demons, the tzitzimime have rattlesnakes dangling between their legs. This appendage can attack just like a normal rattler (see *The Marshal's Guide*).

　Shapechanging: Tzitzimime can assume the shape of any beast.

　Gruesomeness: A tzitzimime's appearance requires anyone who sees it to make an Onerous (7) *guts* check each round for 1d4 rounds.

　Undead.

Description: Tzitzimime look like skeletal humans, perhaps with a few scraps of flesh clinging to the tops of their skulls (never around the jaws) or elsewhere. At every joint they have a tiny skeletal mouth and eyes. Their limbs end in claws instead of normal hands and feet, and they have rattlesnakes for private parts. Their hair is wildly disarranged, their earrings are human hands, and they wear a necklace of bloody human hearts alternating with hands

PRONUNCIATION GUIDE

Some of the Aztec and Spanish words found in this book are a lot to try to get your tongue around. Here's a quick pronunciation guide:

Word Pronunciation

Anahuac
  Ah-NA-hwak
Atlatl
  At-LAT-ul
Ayuntamiento
  Ah-yoont-ah-mee-EN-toe
Baluarte
  Bal-oo-ART-tay
Caballero
  Kah-bah-YAIR-o
Calpulli
  Kal-POOL-li
Cenote
  Seh-NO-tay
Cerro de Chapulín
  SAIR-roe day chap-oo-LEEN
Chalchiutlicue
  Chal-chee-oot-LEE-koo
Chantico
  Shan-TEE-koe
Cihuateteo
  See-hwa-tay-TAY-o
Cimarrone
  See-mah-ROE-nay
Cipactli
  See-PAHK-tlee
Coatlicue
  KWAT-lee-koo-ay
Conquistador
  Kon-KEES-ta-door
Criollo
  Kree-O-yo
Ejército De Los Muertos
  Eh-HAIR-see-toe Day Loase MWAIR-toase
Encomienda
  En-ko-mee-END-da
Fuero
  FWAIR-o
Hacienda
  Ha-see-END-da
Hermanos
  Air-MAHN-noas

Huehuecoyotl
  Hway-hway-koy-YOE-tul
Huei Tlatoani
  HWAY tlah-toe-AN-ee
Huitzilopochtli
  Hweet-zeel-o-POTCH-tlee
Ichcauipilli
  Itch-cow-ee-PILL-ee
Iturbide
  It-tour-BEE-day
Itzacíhuatl
  Its-zak-ee-HWA-tul
Iztlecuhtle
  Iz-tlay-KOOT-lay
Iztli
  IZ-tlee
Juárez
  HWA-rez
Macahuitl
  Ma-kuh-HWEE-tul
Mestizo
  Mess-TEE-zo
Mictlan
  MEEK-tlahn
Mictlantecuhtli
  Meek-tlahn-tay-KOOT-lee
Mixcoatl
  Mish-KWA-tul
Nahual
  NAH-hwal
Nahuatl
  Nah-HWA-tul
Nanahuatzin
  Nah-nah-HWATT-zeen
Oaxaca
  Wa-HA-kuh
Ometecuhtli
  Oh-may-tay-KOOT-lee
Opoche
  Oh-POE-chay
Otontin
  Oh-TAHN-teen
Patecatl
  Pah-tay-KOT-tul
Peninsulare
  Pen-in-soo-LAR-ray
Piedras Gemiras
  Pee-AID-rahs Hem-EER-ahs
Popocatépetl
  Po-po-kah-TAY-petul
Quachic
  KAY-cheek

Quetl Tloque Nahua
  KAY-tul TLO-kay NAH-hwa
Quetzalcoatl
  Kate-zel-KWA-tul
Tapatíos
  Tah-puh-TEE-ose
Tecpatl
  Tek-PAH-tul
Tenochtitlan
  Tay-notch-TEET-lan
Teochcautin
  Tee-otch-COW-tin
Teotihuacán
  Tay-o-tee-hwa-CAHN
Texcoco
  Tesh-KO-ko
Tezcatlipoca
  Tez-kat-lee-PO-ka
Tezontle
  Tez-ON-tlay
Tlacopan
  Tlah-CO-pan
Tlaloc
  TLAH-lock
Tlaltecuhtli
  Tlal-tay-KOOT-lee
Tlatelolco
  Tlah-tay-LOL-ko
Tlazolteotl
  Tlah-zole-tee-OH-tul
Tlauiztli
  Tlow-IZ-tlee
Tzitzimime
  Zeet-zee-MEE-may
Tzompantli
  Zom-PANT-lee
Veracruz
  Bay-rah-KROOS
Xibalbá
  Shee-ball-BAH
Xitlan
  SHEET-lan
Xipe Totec
  SHIE-pay TOE-tek
Xiuhcoatl
  Shoo-KWA-tul
Xiuhtecuhtli
  Shoo-tay-KOOT-lee
Xochipilli
  Sho-chee-PEEL-lee
Xochiquetzal
  Sho-chee-KET-zahl
Xochiyaoyotl
  Show-chee-YOW-yo-tul
Zócalo
  ZO-cull-o

Issue #6
Character Info, Errata, and The Big Picture of the Deadlands Universe

Welcome to Pinnacle's regular update on the Deadlands universe. In this issue we talk about the latest events in the Great Rail Wars and some of Gomorra's seedier inhabitants.

Rail Gangs Battle in Wyoming

After a few relatively quiet months, the war between the Rail Barons has flared again, this time near the tiny, remote town of Bitter Creek, Wyoming, a small settlement roughly 200 miles west of Cheyenne. The battle near this little town involved the troops of three railroads—Iron Dragon, Union Blue, and Wasatch—and the forces of the Reverend Grimme.

According to the inhabitants of Bitter Creek, Kang's troops were the first on the scene. Shortly after their arrival, rail workers accompanying the Iron Dragon thugs began excavating a large mound to the west of town. The townsfolk were unable to get a good look at exactly what Kang's men were up to, because the site of the dig was heavily guarded. Some witnesses reported seeing large, pale-skinned creatures with a single eye and bright, blue hair wandering around in the Iron Dragon camp.

A few days after the arrival of Kang's forces, those of Grimme and Union Blue showed up on the scene. The two groups of newcomers made camp just out of sight of the Iron Dragon encampment.

Over the next few days, the three groups skirmished briefly with each other, but none of them were willing to commit to a full-scale assault. This three-way standoff might have gone on for weeks, or at least until Kang's men found whatever it was they had come for, but the delicate balance of forces was suddenly shattered by the arrival of the Wasatch troops.

Charge!

In the early hours of the stalemate's fifth day, the inhabitants of Bitter Creek were awoken by the screech of steam whistles and the loud clanking of metal on metal. The bleary-eyed townspeople stumbled out of bed to their windows in time to see a column of Wasatch troops pass through town. What they saw was both amazing and frightening.

In addition to the normal rank-and-file troops like X-squads, automatons, and clockwork tarantulas—terrifying enough to those unacquainted with them—Hellstromme's soldiers were equipped with his latest invention for the battlefields of the Rail Wars: the steam spider. These fearsome vehicles resemble enormous, mechanical, steam-powered spiders.

These awe-inspiring devices, most of which stood over twenty feet tall, clumped through town on their heavy, ghost-steel legs, rattling windows and knocking items of off shelves, and made straight for the Iron Dragon camp.

The arachnid juggernauts, belching flame and bullets, smashed through the Iron Dragon defenses like an enraged bull through a barn door. The surprised defenders scattered before the steam spiders' onslaught, leaving the site of their digging completely unguarded. The few defenders who stood against them, including the strange, pale-skinned creatures, were cut down in a hail of bullets or trampled beneath the contraptions' heavy iron feet.

Once Kang's men were routed, the Wasatch forces occupied the camp and set to work continuing the excavation. A few of the vehicles which were part of Hellstromme's attack force were specially outfitted with heavy digging equipment; in a few hours they accomplished more than Kang's men had in days.

Bloodbath

Of course, this wasn't the end of the battle by a long shot. The Iron Dragon forces regrouped and counterattacked. Once the fighting at the dig site began again, both the Union Blue troops and Grimme's lackeys decided this was their best opportunity to get their licks in, and they attacked also.

The battle degenerated into a swirling melee in which each side fought all of the others. The troops of two factions occasionally combined forces to defeat the troops of a third, but as soon as the threat was dealt with, the two allies would turn on each other.

The battle raged for another two hours. It finally ended when a shell from Union Blue artillery pierced the boiler of one of the Wasatch spiders. The resulting explosion ripped the contraption apart and sent red-hot shrapnel flying through the ranks of the troops fighting around it. All of the factions involved took heavy losses from this and fell back to lick their wounds.

Escape

That night, the Wasatch forces retreated under the cover of darkness. The other factions, all of which had large numbers of wounded, declined to pursue Hellstromme's troops. The next morning the three remaining armies slowly edged their way away from the battlefield, keeping a cautious eye cocked in the direction of their enemies.

An Empty Hole

Once the Rail Baron's forces had left the area, some of the more adventurous residents of Bitter Creek decided to have a look at the site of Iron Dragon's digging and find out exactly what the battle had been about. At the center of the campsite, surrounded by twisted wreckage and mangled bodies, they found a deep hole in the ground. At the bottom of the hole was what a stone chamber which had obviously been carved out of the rock by hand. There were deep grooves in the chamber's floor as if some heavy object had once rested there, but whatever made the grooves was gone. Whether it was taken by the retreating Wasatch troopers, or they left as empty-handed as the other factions is unknown.

Even though we added an extra 16 pages to *Doomtown or Bust*, we still couldn't fit in all the desperadoes that inhabit that forsaken pesthole. Here are a few that didn't make the first cut.

The Agency

With all the supernatural shenanigans that are going on in Gomorra, it's only natural that the Agency should send a few operatives to check things out.

Johnny Quaid

The Ghost has sent Johnny—a large man and a born miner—to infiltrate the Sweetrock mines, watching for signs of supernatural activity there. Quaid has quickly established a network of contacts and informants among the miners, and he's done his best to assuage their fears of the unknown. He hasn't been able to stem the growing tide of fear, but he has pegged a few supernatural hiding holes in the area and sent his Agency contacts in to clean house. He's also in a good position to discover Sweetrock's plans for the mines.

Profile: Johnny Quaid

Corporeal: D:2d8 N:3d6 Q:2d6 S:2d12 V:5d10
Climbin' 1d6, fightin': brawlin', pick-ax 4d6, shootin': pistol, automatics 3d8, throwin': unbalanced 2d8, sneak 3d6, swimmin' 2d6
Mental: C:2d10 K:1d6 M:2d8 Sm:2d8 Sp:3d10
Academia: occult 3d6, demolition 3d6, gamblin' 2d8, search 2d10, trade: mining 4d6
Edges: Big ears 1, brawny 3, friends in high places (the Agency) 3
Hindrances: Loyal (Agency) –3, obligation (to keep his miner friends safe) –3
Gear: Pick, rowboat, lantern, Gatling pistol, box of 50 shells.

Cort Williams

Cort was working the Fellheimer's Folly case when the Ghost pulled him for duties in Gomorra. He's an experienced gunfighter with an odd tendency for tidiness that makes him a perfect Agency man. He never likes to see a mess go un-cleaned for long, and Gomorra's about the biggest he's ever seen. Before entering a Pinkerton operation, he always puts on a pair of black leather gloves, to keep himself sanitary.

Profile: Cort Williams

Corporeal: D:3d8 N:2d10 Q:4d6 S:1d10 V:2d6
Climbin' 1d10, fightin': brawlin' 2d10, lockpickin' 2d8, shootin': pistol 4d8, sneak 3d10
Mental: C:2d12 K:2d8 M:3d10 Sm:3d8 Sp:2d6
Academia: occult 3d8, bluff 2d10, guts 2d6 overawe 3d10, persuasion 2d10, scrutinize 3d12, search 5d12, streetwise 3d8
Edges: Brave 2
Hindrances: Habit (neatness) –2, loyal (Agency) –3, tinhorn –2
Gear: Gatling pistol, 50 shells, long duster.

Black Jacks

The Black Jacks also have it in for Sweetrock Mining, but for completely different reasons.

Lawrence Goodman

Lawrence is a disgruntled employee, distrustful of his bank for cozying up to Sweetrock and desperate to think of some way

to make them pay. When Black Jack made him an offer, he jumped at the chance. Now, with the bank robbery behind him, he hopes to be of further use to the gang by filtering information and serving as their eyes and ears in Gomorra. Besides getting to stick it to Sweetrock, Black Jack pays a lot better, too.

Profile: Lawrence Goodman

Corporeal: D:2d8 N:3d8 Q:3d6 S:2d6 V:2d6
Climbin' 1d8, filchin' 2d8, horse ridin' 2d8, lockpickin' 2d8, shootin': pistols 2d8, sneak 2d8
Mental: C:3d8 K:3d6 M:2d6 Sm:2d6 Sp:3d6
Persuasion 2d6, scrutinize 3d8, trade: banking 3d6
Gear: bank keys, .38 pistol, 20 shells.

Sam Horowitz

Sam was crazy enough to rob the railroads as they pushed their way west, and he has antagonized just about every participant in the Great Rail Wars at one time or another. He lit out for California when the heat got too much. The fact that he made it to Gomorra alive was enough to convince Black Jack to sign him on.

Profile: Sam Horowitz

Corporeal: D:2d10 N:3d8 Q:2d8 S:4d6 V:3d6
Climbin' 1d8, dodge 2d8, fightin': brawlin' 3d8, horse ridin' 2d8, shootin': pistol 4d10, sneak 4d8, swimmin' 2d8
Mental: C:3d10 K:2d6 M:3d6 Sm:2d8 Sp:2d6
Demolition 5d6, guts 4d6, scrutinize 2d10, search 3d10, streetwise 3d8, trade: railroads 3d6
Edges: Big ears 1, nerves o' steel 1
Hindrances: Outlaw –4, enemy –5 (many many railroad companies)
Gear: Colt Peacemaker, 20 shells, dynamite, coils of fuses, matches, bowler derby, black handkerchief.

Maze Rats

Kang's boys continue to wreak havoc.

Mitobu

This truly bizarre man claims to be a native of the South Seas and speaks with a perfect Polynesian accent—even though he's as white a sheet. His well-muscled body is completely hairless and scarred with ritualistic patterns. His specialty is harpooning—either other ships or abominations that get too close. He proudly operates the *Typhoon's* harpoon rig.

Profile: Mitobu

Corporeal: D:3d12 N:4d6 Q:2d6 S:4d10 V:5d10
Climbin' 1d6, drivin': boat 2d6, fightin': brawlin' 3d6, shootin': harpoon 5d12, swimmin' 3d6, throwin': unbalanced 4d12
Mental: C:3d10 K:1d4 M:2d6 Sm:2d6 Sp:3d8
Artillery 3d10, guts 4d8, language: English 2d4, overawe 4d6, search 2d10
Edges: Brawny 3, "the stare" 1, thick-skinned 3
Hindrances: Ferner -3, outlaw -3
Gear: Many harpoons, tow cables.

Marko Muscovich

A Russian expatriate, Marko is charged with maintaining the Typhoon's ghost rock engines and sails. He often swings from the mast during attacks on other ships, dropping down on unsuspecting crewmen from above. His knowledge of shipbuilding lets him find the best places to hole an enemy vessel—such that they'll sink without the Rats having to board.

Profile: Marko Muscovich

Corporeal: D:3d8 N:2d8 Q:3d6 S:3d8 V:2d10
Climbin 5d8, dodge 4d8, drivin': boat 3d8, fightin': brawlin', sword 4d8, shootin': shotgun 3d8, sneak 2d8, swimmin' 3d8, throwin': balanced 4d8
Mental: C:2d10 K:2d6 M:1d6 Sm:2d6 Sp:2d6
Artillery 3d10, bluff 2d6, gamblin' 2d6, language: English 2d6, overawe 3d6, tinkerin' 3d6
Edges: Fleet-footed 3
Hindrances: Outlaw -3
Gear: Climbing ropes, tools, shotgun, 10 shells, cutlass.

Sioux Union

Joseph Eyes-Like-Rain's followers are keeping a close eye on the mining operations in Gomorra.

Benjamin Nightsinger

Benjamin is a Navajo with a unique background as both an Indian shaman and a white man's priest. He was granted permission by his tribal chief to "study the white man's ways," in an effort to better understand how to defeat the evil which walked the land. He learned from Spanish missionaries, Mormon preachers and traveling Baptists, incorporating their thoughts and beliefs into his own understanding of the world. While never formally ordained, he received a certain amount of faith in his studies without losing the spiritual favor he had held as a Navajo.

Profile: Benjamin Nightsinger

Corporeal: D:3d6 N:3d8 Q:2d8 S:3d6 V:4d6
Climbin' 1d8, fightin': knife 2d8, shootin': pistol 2d6, sneak 2d8
Mental: C:3d8 K:4d6 M:2d6 Sm:3d8 Sp:3d12
Faith 4d12, language: English 4d6, professional: religion 5d6, search 2d8
Edges: Arcane Background: shaman, blessed (unique combination; unavailable to others) 6
Hindrances: Poverty -3
Gear: .38 pistol, ammunition belt, 30 shells, crucifix, medicine bundle.
Special Abilities:
   Shaman 3: Rituals: Dance, tobacco, Favors: Pact, lightning strike, earth Speak
      Blessed: Miracles: Inspiration, lay on hands, smite

Steven S. Long

Steven S. Long is a freelance writer and game designer. Prior to movin' out west to help keep the Fearmongers at bay with such fine tomes as *Law Dogs*, *Tales O' Terror: 1877*, and *Brainburners*, he practiced law Back East in North Carolina.

After taking down his shyster's shingle and setting out to write and design games, he wrote books like *Dark Champions* and *The Ultimate Martial Artist* for Hero Games (for whom he recently finished the long-awaited Fifth Edition of the HERO System), *World of Darkness: Combat* and *Destiny's Price* for White Wolf Game Studios, and many other products designed to help fine folks while away a few hours.

Recently he's been takin' trips out among the stars in his job as general roustabout for Last Unicorn Games's *Star Trek* game lines, including becoming Line Developer for the *Star Trek: Deep Space Nine Roleplaying Game*.

In northern Arizona, there is a gash in the earth, a wound of unparalleled size and depth. The native peoples call it the House of Stone and Light. Explorers and settlers call it the Grand Canyon.

But the canyon hold an ancient secret, one that certain people will kill to possess—or die to protect.

CANYON O' DOOM